1 9 3 4

1 9 8 4

WNEW · WHERE THE

MELODY LINGERS ON

CONCEIVED, WRITTEN, DESIGNED AND PUBLISHED BY
NIGHTINGALE GORDON, NEW YORK

TO THE WNEW FAMILY,
PAST AND PRESENT.
TO YOU, AND YOU,
AND ESPECIALLY YOU.

John W. Kluge, Chairman and President of Metromedia, Inc., received a B.A. degree from Columbia University in 1937 and, in the same year, joined Otten Brothers Co., Detroit paper converters. Within four years he became a vice president and part owner of the firm. Following his military service, Mr. Kluge sold his Otten interest and moved to Washington, D.C. where in 1946, with a partner, he founded station WGAY Radio in Silver Spring, Md.

Mr. Kluge formed the New England Fritos Corporation in 1947 and four years later founded a food brokerage firm, Kluge and Co. This was expanded in 1956 through the formation of Kluge, Finkelstein and Co. in Baltimore, in partnership with David Finkelstein. Subsequently, Mr. Kluge served as a marketing consultant to some of America's leading packaged foods producers.

In January 1959, Mr. Kluge joined Metropolitan Broadcasting Corporation and became Chief Executive Officer. At that time, the company consisted of two television and four radio stations. Following the acquisition of Foster & Kleiser's outdoor advertising operations and a number of additional television and radio stations, the company's name was changed to Metromedia, Inc. in 1961, to reflect the growing scope and diversity of its activities.

Today, Metromedia, Inc. is the nation's leading independent broadcaster and outdoor advertising company. During the broadcast week, Metromedia's television and radio stations reach more homes in the United States than any other broadcasting group with the exception of the three major networks. Foster & Kleiser is the leader in the outdoor advertising industry. Metromedia's entertainment division encompasses television program production and distribution, as well as the world-famous Harlem Globetrotters and the Ice Capades. In the field of telecommunications, Metromedia is a leading radio common carrier in the United States.

Metromedia Radio is the nation's leading independent group broadcaster, operating both AM and FM stations in ten major U.S. metropolitan areas. Although Metromedia's radio stations vary in format from rock to all-news, each one uniformly communicates information of local interest and importance to listeners.

WNEW is the flagship station of Metromedia, Inc. With the support and guidance of John W. Kluge, WNEW continues to be one of the most listened to adult music radio stations in metropolitan New York.

In addition to his responsibilities with Metromedia, Inc., Mr. Kluge is a director of The Shubert Foundation, The United Cerebral Palsy Associations, Inc., Armand Hammer College: The United World College of the American West, CONAIR, Waldorf-Astoria Corporation, Chock Full O'Nuts Corporation, Westmount International Hotels, Inc., and Just One Break, Inc. He is a Governor of the New York College of Osteopathic Medicine, as well as a Trustee of the Preventive Medicine Institute—Strang Clinic, a member of the Advisory Committee of Manufacturers Hanover Trust Company, a member of the Board of Governors of the Metropolitan Club, and a Trustee of the Skowhegan School of Painting and Sculpture.

Mr. Kluge's numerous honors and awards include Knight of the Order of Sant'Agata; INTV Award (Independent Television Association) for Outstanding Leadership in Independent Television; Man of the Year Award, Catholic Relief Services; John Jay Award, Columbia College, New York; Humanitarian Award, United Cerebral Palsy of New York City; Gold Medal Award, International Radio and Television Society; Man of the Year Award, The Bedside Network; Honorary Degree, Doctor of Laws, College of Mount St. Vincent; Honorary Degree, Doctor of Laws, New York Institute of Technology; Distinguished Public Service Award, Anti-Defamation League; and Man of the Year Award, New York Association for the Blind.

JOHN W. KLUGE
Chairman and President of Metromedia, Inc.

The 50th anniversary of WNEW is a celebration of our past and a fanfare for our future. We're proud of what has come before and of the wonderful people who have made it all possible.

We honor the on-air personalities whose voices and talent have created the unmistakable sound of WNEW.

We recognize the commitment of the dedicated men and women who have worked to make WNEW the best radio station in the country.

We salute the artists who have sung the songs and played the music which have made us famous. For half a century, WNEW has been the station of the stars.

And most of all, we appreciate you—our loyal listeners. You have danced to our music, applauded our triumphs, and taken us to your hearts.

I am honored to preside over the renaissance of WNEW as we reclaim a long and beloved musical past. WNEW is where it all began, and we are proud to be the standard bearer for the best in classic American music.

JACK THAYER
Vice President and General Manager of WNEW

THE PIER WAS CROWDED THAT morning. Among the arriving passengers was Bernice Judis, returning to New York after several months in Europe. The only daughter of a wealthy New York real estate man, Judis grew up in the Twenties with all the social advantages of a well-bred young woman. She attended the better class of speakeasies, went to parties, and became golf champion of New Jersey.

Waiting on the dock was her old friend Sophie Biow. Mrs. Biow had decided that Judis was wasting her considerable, but undeveloped, talents.

"Tudie," cried Sophie. "Welcome home. We've got a job for you. Milton and Arde Bulova have just bought this little radio station, and you can help put it together."

"But I've never worked a day in my life."

"Don't worry, darling. We'll show you."

S OPHIE'S HUSBAND, ADVERTIS-ing executive Milton Biow, and Arde Bulova, manufacturer of watches, had recently acquired two small radio stations from the Amalgamated Broadcasting System. The ABS, formed by comedian Ed Wynn to challenge the three major radio networks, had failed, and Biow and Bulova took over five floors of studios at 501 Madison Avenue.

Ed Wynn's initials are often said to be the source of WNEW's call letters. But retired engineer John Zarpaylic offers this first-hand account: "One Sunday morning I had to drive Mr. Biow and Richard O'Dea [owner of station WODA] to the new location in Carlstadt where they were building the transmitter. And the discussion was, what are we going to call this? Milton Biow said, 'We haven't had a station built in this area since 1928. I think the best call letters we could have are WNEW, which says *new*. New in the metropolitan area. The newest thing in radio.'"

At Sophie's suggestion, Milton Biow asked Bernice Judis to accompany him to the studios in Newark, to wait for the incoming furniture. Tudie agreed, and soon she was hired for $15 a week. She took to authority as naturally as she had taken to golf.

Early broadcasts from WNEW's Newark studios featured the band of staff musicians. Ed Laux, *above,* was the announcer.

I was a teenager, keeping house for my father and two brothers.
On my birthday, November 28, 1934, I was given a small radio.
I turned the dial, found something I liked, WNEW, and never changed stations.
In 1944, my husband, who loved classical music, decided to change stations.
My poor little radio promptly broke.
HARRIET S. PAULSON

Jackie Tamburel was known to radio audiences as *The Little Mona Lisa of the Air.*

"WNEW TO DEFY SUPERSTI-TION," ran the headline in the *New York Evening Journal* on February 6, 1934. The article went on: "The management of WNEW, the newest of the metropolitan broadcasting plants, has an utter disregard for superstition, and will flaunt it to the world by opening WNEW on the evening of February 13. WNEW will, at its inaugural, throw tradition to the winds and make its bow without any guest stars. The premiere will merely feature its own staff of musicians and other artists in a grand review, so that John Q. Public will be able to gather some notion of the calibre of entertainment plotted out by the owners."

WNEW took to the airwaves at 8 P.M. on a Tuesday evening. The first hour was devoted to a review of radio history, with outstanding events dramatized. At 9, President Franklin Roosevelt pressed a button in his White House study which illuminated a golden lamp in the transmitter room. Following the signal from Washington, soprano Yvonne D'Arle sang *The Star-Spangled Banner* and Governor A. Harry Moore of New Jersey delivered an address of welcome. A musical review followed, featuring choruses, mountaineers, harmony groups, and sports announcers. The Kilocycle Club with Zoel Parento and the staff orchestra presented a program designed to popularize the 1250

WNEW Makes Bow Tuesday Evening

WNEW, newest regional station in the metropolitan area, goes on the air Tuesday evening at 8, it was announced today by Milton Biow, president. The opening ceremonies, with the exception of dedicatory speeches by public officials, will feature only artists scheduled to be heard regularly over WNEW.

WNEW will operate on 1250 kilocycles ... the daytime ...

FIRST BROADCAST TODAY.

Radio Station WNEW to Be Opened When Roosevelt Presses Button.

Station WNEW, the latest addition to the ranks of metropolitan broadcasters, opens tonight at 8 o'clock. President Roosevelt has been invited to press a button in his study in the White House at 9 P.M., which will illuminate a lamp at the transmitter in Carlstadt, N.J.

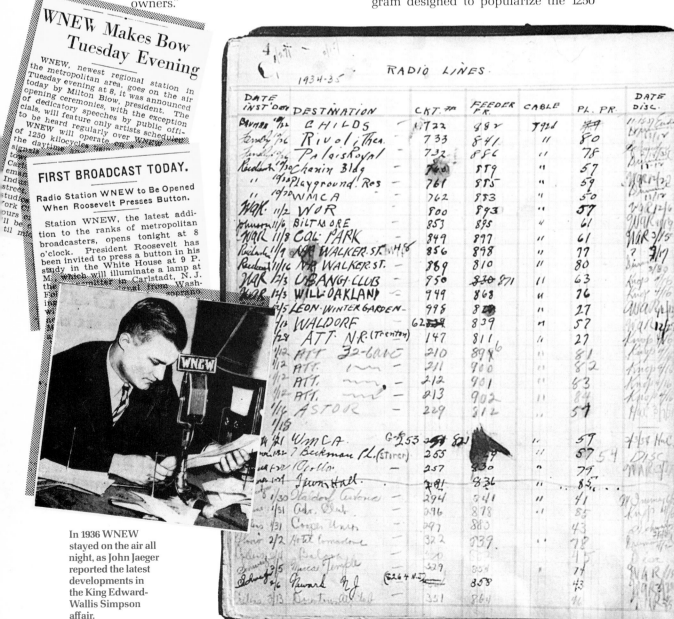

In 1936 WNEW stayed on the air all night, as John Jaeger reported the latest developments in the King Edward-Wallis Simpson affair.

In the late Thirties, my sister got a Silvertone table radio for her birthday. It had pushbuttons on it, and she wrote away to Sears and got four little WNEW stickers to paste on the buttons— she had them all tuned to WNEW.

DANIEL B. HOOVEN

kilocycle wavelength.

Broadcast signals radiated from a 424-foot tower near the transmitter. WNEW's transmitter, originally owned by the Columbia Broadcasting System, had been located in Wayne, N.J. It was taken apart and reassembled in Carlstadt by engineer Max Weiner. WNEW operated on a 1250 kilocycle frequency using 2500 watts in the daytime and 1000 at night. Programs emanated from studios in the Industrial Office Building in Newark and from auxiliary facilities at 501 Madison Avenue. The station was on the air from 7 A.M. until midnight, with the exception of a few hours on Sunday afternoon and Monday evening.

WNEW presented a varied program during its first week of operation. In accordance with its announced policy of broadcasting as many sports events as possible, WNEW ran live coverage of the Tilden–Vines tennis match in Philadelphia on Friday night, February 16. On Saturday evening, a program dedicated to the mayor of Newark featured soprano Jackie Tamburel, known as *The Little Mona Lisa of the Air*. A live orchestra performed in the Newark studio with vocalist Theresa Stabile, who later went on to fame as Dolly Dawn and her Dawn Patrol. Kay Reed, former organist at the Roxy Theater, signed on in the early days and remained house organist for many years.

Faith Fortune, one of radio's first advice columnists, reminded WNEW listeners that "where there's life, there's hope."

As a young teenager back in the Thirties, I remember Martin Block's Make Believe Ballroom playing on many radios in the building I lived in. Most people kept their doors open in those days and the wonderful Big Band music permeated the air.
JIM MASCIA

Biow and Bulova, occupied with their own growing businesses, appointed Bernice Judis General Manager less than a year after she joined WNEW. With no previous experience in radio, she soon discovered she had a talent for programming. As Jim Lowe remarks, "She knew, she just instinctively knew."

IN THE MID-THIRTIES, THE RADIO industry was dominated by the network giants which were just approaching the height of their power. Independent WNEW competed with the programming strength of the Columbia Broadcasting System, the Mutual Broadcasting System, and two branches of the National Broadcasting Company, the Red which remained NBC and the Blue which later became the American Broadcasting Company. Network radio in the Thirties was similar to network television today, and programs followed a set pattern. The day began with a cheerful morning show, followed by recipes, soap operas, noon news, more soap operas, organ interludes, children's shows, and sports events. Evenings were dominated by elaborate music and comedy shows featuring established stars like Jack Benny, Georgie Jessel, Buddy Rogers, and Rudy Vallee.

Bernice Judis lacked the budget to match these programs, but more important, she found them boring and unappealing. She felt that women listening at home were sated with the "tune in tomorrow and learn if Gwendolyn's sweetheart ran off with her best friend" diet of soap operas. And she was of the firm belief that "a woman who has to boil the beef doesn't necessarily want to hear about it on the radio." Judis countered serials and recipes with a flow of lively popular recorded music, providing welcome distraction for thousands of housewives. Suddenly, WNEW's ratings began to climb, as New Yorkers discovered a new kind of radio fare.

BERNICE JUDIS WAS A BRILliant, dedicated administrator, determined to make WNEW the best independent radio station in the country. Uncompromising in her adherence to the highest standards and keenly aware of public tastes, she drew an enormous audience to the station. Through innovative programming and the recruitment of popular on-air personalities, Judis successfully rivaled the networks and created a formula for independent radio which revolutionized the industry.

John Van Buren Sullivan has known Judis since he joined the sales staff in 1942, later succeeding her as General Manager. In describing the influence Judis had on station personnel, Sullivan says, "You couldn't help but benefit because she challenged you, she dared you, she rewarded you, she complimented you and she understood...she got the best out of you." Bernice Judis was intimately involved in every aspect of running the station, holding morning coffee *klatches* with salesmen, coaching and prodding announcers, proclaiming her opinions with outspoken passion.

Nevertheless, she was always willing to experiment. Sullivan explains that "it

SOON AFTER SHE BECAME GENERAL MANAGER OF WNEW, BERNICE JUDIS CHANGED THE NATURE OF RADIO WITH INNOVATIVE PROGRAMMING.

I have been listening to WNEW all my life since we were both born in 1934. My earliest recollection is of my sister singing along with Martin Block's Ballroom with her song sheet, and my wishing I could read.
MILLIE CANCRO

wasn't just looking for somebody new, it was looking for somebody good so that the listeners could benefit. Somebody could have 800 solid gold records in Australia, and if he came in here sounding like a kangaroo with a bad cold, she'd say get lost." Her instincts changed the nature of radio, giving Martin Block the opportunity to become America's first disc jockey and nurturing the unconventional style of Gene Rayburn and Dee Finch. She initiated the first all-night radio show, originated news around the clock, and brought unknown announcers to WNEW who went on to become the best-known personalities in radio.

"I love radios like some men love cars," Bernice Judis once said. She had a radio in every room in her house, in every office at the station, and even carried a small portable in her purse. Judis constantly monitored WNEW's broadcasts, never hesitating to telephone the studio with praise or, more often, criticism. A disc jockey speaking too loudly at 3 A.M. might receive a call to "please pipe down." She liked to think of herself as an average listener, giving vent to her exasperation.

Bernice Judis was a colorful woman who embellished her relentless ambition with expensive clothing, spectacular jewelry, and heavy perfumes. She occasionally delighted in the shock of outrageous behavior. Yet as one of the few women prominent in broadcasting, she commanded tremendous respect. Ethel Eisenberg, who came to fame in the Forties as singer Ann Perry, tells of the time that Golda Meir and Eleanor Roosevelt visited the station. "They

were sitting in her office and saying, 'We compliment you, we've never known a woman who runs a successful business all on her own.'" Bernice Judis remained at the station for twenty years, and under her guidance WNEW became one of the most successful independent stations in the history of radio.

Organist Kay Reed remembers Judis from the beginning: "We were a big family. We all worked together, one for the other. But I'll tell you frankly, it was Miss Judis that held us together. She was the spark of the whole thing."

The successful
WNEW team,
from top:
Bobbie Godet,
Jimmy Rich,
Marion Joyce,
Bernice Judis,
Lanny Grey.

"MR. BLOCK OF CALIFORNIA TO SEE you, Miss Judis." Amused and intrigued, she agreed to give the young announcer an audition. After Martin Block read the straight commercials, she handed him a pencil to describe. Block kept talking about the pencil for twenty minutes and was hired as a part-time announcer at the salary of $25 a week.

Colonel Charles Lindbergh was a national hero, the first man to fly alone across the Atlantic. The nation was shocked when his infant son was kidnapped and later found murdered. When Bruno Richard Hauptmann was accused of the crime and brought to trial, the country followed the proceedings on a day-to-day basis through radio, newspapers, magazines, and newsreels. Bernice Judis decided to present live remote coverage of the trial, and a reporter and an engineer were sent to Flemington, N.J., where they broadcast from a men's room in the courthouse. A vast New York audience sat fascinated by WNEW's reports, the only coverage from inside the building.

Naturally, there were long periods of time between bulletins, and Martin Block suggested that he fill the gaps with recorded music played by the nation's leading bands. Judis agreed, and within half an hour Block had bought six records from the corner music store. On February 3, 1935, *Make Believe Ballroom* was on the air.

IN THE EARLY DAYS OF RADIO, recorded music gave studio musicians time to rehearse between live performances. "At the time that Martin came upon the scene," William B. Williams explains, "most announcers used to cup their hands over their ears, and their enunciation was brilliant, but you never got the feeling in listening to them that they were human. He was the first to say, 'I'm just another fellow, I might be the fellow next door, and I want to talk to you'…and he did it beautifully." Block was the first announcer to personalize records, inspiring Walter Winchell to coin the phrase *disc jockey*.

"A record is a record no matter whose program it plays on," states Joe Franklin, who began his career as Block's record picker, "but somehow when Martin Block would introduce a record with his wit, his voice, that same record had some new magical lustre." Block's intimate style captivated listeners, and from a 15-minute experimental program, the show was quickly expanded to 90 minutes, winning immediate success. *Make Believe Ballroom* heralded a new era in broadcasting.

Block's starting salary was recorded in the original WNEW payroll book.

My memories of WNEW go back to Martin Block, starting in 1936. Conventional wisdom had it that if you could pick 30 songs and one became a hit, you would succeed as a music publisher. I thought I was the greatest business brain since F.W. Woolworth, because more than half the songs I liked became hits. Little did I realize that by the time a song made it to the Make Believe Ballroom, it was well on the way to becoming a hit.

JAMES F. SELIGMAN

IT'S MAKE BELIEVE
BALLROOM TIME,
PUT ALL YOUR CARES AWAY.
ALL THE BANDS ARE HERE,
TO BRING GOOD CHEER
YOUR WAY.
IT'S MAKE BELIEVE
BALLROOM TIME,
THE HOUR OF SWEET ROMANCE,
HERE'S YOUR MAKE
BELIEVE BALLROOM,
COME ON, CHILDREN,
LET'S DANCE!
LET'S DANCE!

Music by Harold Green. Lyrics by Mickey Stoner and
Martin Block. Recorded by Glenn Miller.

The format of the program never changed. Employing the gentle fiction that each record was a live performance, Block welcomed popular bands and singers to an imaginary ballroom with a revolving stage. Each performer stayed under the crystal chandelier for 15 minutes. Millions of people visualized the ballroom in the theater of their imagination.

"He had a feel for the ear of New York that was remarkable," observes Williams. "Martin had an uncanny ability to know what kind of music, which bands, which new releases would be the ones that would satisfy the public."

This ability gained him considerable influence. Block's Friday night previews of new releases, Saturday morning top-20 countdowns, and the semi-annual popularity polls carried enormous weight with listeners, artists, and record companies. Programs like *Make Believe Ballroom* seemed to create hit records, and disc jockeys soon became the major promotion channel for the phonograph industry.

AT THE HEIGHT OF ITS POPUlarity *Make Believe Ballroom* commanded an astonishing 25% of the listening audience against strong network competition. Block once estimated that he played 365,000 records during the 21,500 hours he hosted the *Ballroom*. In addition to presenting the Big Band sound to a vast radio audience, Block emceed live shows and broadcasts from places such as the Glen Island Casino. His fame approached that of the artists whose music he loved.

Away from the spotlight, Martin Block revealed a less serious side. He delighted in strolling off the elevator as the *Ballroom* theme was playing, reaching the microphone just as the music ended. A barber might be giving him a shave in the studio and as a record ended, Block stood up with lather on his face and a sheet around him to deliver the commercial. Country star Zeke Manners once gave Block his cowboy hat and for months Martin came to work wearing the hat and toy holsters. As Franklin remembers, Martin Block was "a great practical joker, he never grew up, and he loved life."

The first theme music for *Make Believe Ballroom* was *Sugar Blues* by Clyde McCoy, who had a band in the Midwest when Block introduced his music to New York. Later, the theme became Charlie Barnet's *Make Believe Ballroom*. Glenn Miller, winner of the 1940 popularity poll, recorded *It's Make Believe Ballroom Time*, and following Miller's death in World War II, his close friend Block announced that hereafter the theme would never change.

rtin Block And The Top Tunes Of The Week Of

23. Have A Good Time-
22. The Ruby And The Pearl-
21. Takes Two To Tango-
20. I Laughed At Love-
19. You'll NeverGet Away-
18. Should I-
17. Because Your Mine-
16. Lady Of Spain-
15. String Along-
14. Botch-A-Me-
13. Feet Up-
12. Somewhere Along The Way-
11. Indian Love Call-
10. Glow Worm-
9. High Noon-
8. Half As Much-
7. Jambalaya-
6. Trying-
   -werdemseh'n Sweetheart-
      -llaghan-

-Tony Bennett(was22)
-Nat"King"Cole(new)
-Pearl Baily(new)
-Sonny Gale(was21)
-Don Cornell & Ter
-Four Aces(was14)
-Mario Lanza(was
-EddieFisher(was
-The AMES Brot
-Rosemary Cloon
-Guy Mitchell(
-Nat "King" Co
-Slim Whitman(
-The MILLS Br
Frankie Lai
Rosema

MALE VOCA
1 ALAN DALE
2 PERRY COMO
3 JULIUS LAR
4 EDDIE FISH
5 TONY BENNE
6 JONNIE RAY

MARTIN BLOCK A

3. Be Anything----
.All of Me---
This is the Beg
Sinner Am I---
gh Noon---
ke Rings----s
in a While---
My Heart---
You Were Her
ush---

12th Annual Popularity
Poll - Make-Believe
Ballroom - WNEW

1. Glenn Miller
2. Tommy Dorsey
3. Harry James
4. Jimmy Dorsey
5. Vaughn Monroe
6. Sammy Kaye
7. Benny Goodman
8. Artie Shaw
9. Johnny Long
10. Count Basie
11. Claude Thornhill
12. Charlie Spivak
13. Gene Krupa
14. Woody Herman
15. Charlie Barnet
16. Alvino Rey
17. Xavier Cugat
18. Kay Kyser
19. Guy Lombardo
20. Bob Chester

RESULTS OF MAKE BELIEVE BALLROOM

MALE VOCALISTS   FEMALE VOC

PERRY COMO   1 PATTI PAGE
EDDIE FISHER   2 JONI JAMES
TONY BENNETT   √3 KITTY KALEN
NNIE RAY   4 TERESA
RANK SINATRA   5 DO
N CORNELL
IUS LA ROSA
AN DALE
COLE
DAMONE

RESULTS OF

MALE VOCA
1 TONY BENN
2 PERRY COM
3 EDDIE FISH
4 JON

February, 28,1953

Buddy Morrow(same)
Julius La Rosa(wer
Artie Wayne(new)
Eddie Fisher(was
Frankie Laine(was
Les Paul-Mary Fo
Guy Mitchell(was
Tommy Edwards(w
Perry Como(N E
Joni James(was
Ralph Materie(w
Sunny Gale(was

WNEW

Best wishes to
you and
Respfully your
Martin Block

Here is the
First 20 ba
Popularity (
ed by Martin
MAKE BELIEVE

1. Tommy Dorse
2. Glen Miller
3. Jimmy Dorsey
4. Vaughn Monroe
5. Benny Goodman
6. Sammy Kaye
7. Artie Shaw
8. Harry James
9. Gene Krupa
10. Alvino Rey
11. Count Basie
12. Charlie Barnet
    Will Bradley
    ohnny Long
    arlie Spivak
    y Kyser
    oody Herman
    y Lombardo
    ier Cugat
    Ellington
    WNEW
    ison Avenue
    lew York

The Make Believe Ballroom
Club
1939   1940
WNEW - 501 MADISON AVE. N. Y. C.
Name Edward Emerson
     MEMBER
Address 321 Walnut St. So Amboy NJ
12897
Martin Block
PRESIDENT

NOVEMBER 7,1953

1 EH, CUMPARI-JULIUS LAR
2 YOU, YOU, YOU-THE AMES BA
3 RAGS TO RICHES-TONY BE
4 EBBTIDE-FRANK CHACK
  CON DIOS-LES PAUL-MARY
     -EDDIE FISHER
TONY

THOUSANDS OF
LISTENERS CAST
VOTES IN BLOCK'
SEMI-ANNUAL
POPULARITY POLL
AND EAGERLY
AWAITED THE
RESULTS OF
SATURDAY MORNIN
TOP-20 COUNT-
DOWNS.

THE HEP PARADE OF '49...

with a rousing line-up of top rhythm stars setting the downbeat for love!

See and Hear

FRANKIE LAINE
KING COLE TRIO
TONI HARPER
JACK SMITH
KAY STARR
THE SPORTSMEN
CHARLIE BARNET
JIMMY DORSEY
JAN GARBER
PEE WEE HUNT
GENE KRUPA
RAY McKINLEY

MAKE BELIEVE BALLROOM

with JEROME COURTLAND
RUTH WARRICK
RON RANDELL
VIRGINIA WELLES
AL JARVIS

Screen Play by Albert Duffy
and Karen DeWolf

Story by Albert Duffy

Directed by
Joseph SANTLEY

Produced by
Ted RICHMOND

A COLUMBIA PICTURE

Based on the
radio programs of
AL JARVIS and
MARTIN BLOCK

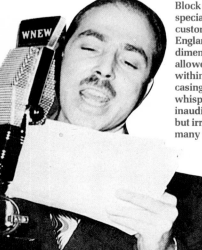

Block devised a special microphone, custom tailored in England to his vocal dimensions, which allowed him to talk within an inch of the casing. His seductive whispers were inaudible in the studio but irresistible to his many listeners.

According to a 1949 review, the film version of *Make Believe Ballroom* featured "one of the jumpin'est jivin'est arrays of rhythm stars in screen history."

…listening to WNEW while growing up in the Israel Orphan Asylum for ten years. The only joy was listening to the radio, and WNEW whenever possible. We would listen to Martin Block and Make Believe Ballroom, and I would dream that I was away from the horrors of the place. The music of WNEW was a lifeline to the rest of the world.
ARLETTE SAS

Block was proud of being "America's super salesman." Sponsors paid a total of $10 million for time on his program, and he was credited with selling $750 million worth of their products. During one month as participating sponsor, Purity Bakers increased sales by 432,000 donuts per week. Writing in *The New York Times* in 1944, John K. Hutchens described Block's unique commercial delivery: "He breathes into the microphone a commercial having to do with fur coats. He does not urge fur coats on his feminine listeners. His voice merely carries an undertone of fervent sympathy for any woman who does not have a fur coat."*

THE ART OF SELLING, WHETHER promoting a performer, introducing a record, or delivering a commercial, was the key to Martin Block's appeal. He left his first job as an office boy at General Electric at 15 because "I wanted to sell things—salesmanship was my life's ambition." Dropping out of school, Block took to selling razor blades and potato peelers on the streets of New York. His first job in radio came at a station in Tijuana, where he delivered commercials. Moving to Los Angeles, Block listened to radio personality Al Jarvis who hosted a show called *Make Believe Ballroom,* and coming to New York, borrowed the program's name. For most of his career at WNEW, Martin Block was on the air for three and a half hours a day, six days a week, with morning and evening editions of the *Ballroom.* He left the station in 1954, moving to ABC with a similar show. From 1961 until his death on Sep-

tember 19, 1967, Block hosted weekend *Hall of Fame* shows on WOR. Block's extensive record collection was donated to New York University.

Block was never able to translate his magic to television. Although he appeared on several programs, he realized his appeal was better suited to radio. Interviewed at the 1954 premiere of *A Star Is Born,* Block said: "Television for some reason spoils a person's ability to use his imagination. And when we lose our imagination, I think we're losing something very important in our lives."

Martin Block played to the imagination. He made each listener feel like an intimate confidant, sharing a special world of music, conversation, and advice. Writing in the February 1937 issue of *Bandstand,* a newspaper published by the Tommy Dorsey band, Block made this prophecy:

"It's your Make Believe Ballroom, You and You and especially You, and it's always been that way as I've stood before the microphones at WNEW introducing the music of the country's leading orchestras, telling about the new recordings and discussing the trend of the moment…I think we'll always have programs like my Make Believe Ballroom—where listeners can hear the best in music…I think it's radio's job to give samples of the music of the modern masters."

BLOCK BROADCAST FROM AN ACTUAL BALLROOM STUDIO, COMPLETE WITH CHANDELIER, RED VELVET CHAIR AND BLACK LINOLEUM ON THE FLOOR.

I remember the Thirties. Martin Block called it Saturday Night in Harlem and we would hear all the black bands—Claude Hopkins, Maxine Sullivan, Duke, Count Basie, Earl Hines.
ED WILLIAMS

THE APPEARANCE OF GLEN GRAY and his Casa Loma Orchestra on the stage of New York's Paramount Theater in December 1935 marked the beginning of the Big Band era. The networks began offering live remotes to satisfy the enormous demand for the new sound. Playing recorded music was the only way for an independent station to survive.

Live music was still important, and WNEW maintained a studio band, the Five Shades of Blue led by Merle Pitt, as well as a house organist. Jimmy Rich, in charge of the music department, scouted for singers to perform with Roy Ross and the studio orchestra. Many newcomers had short-term contracts as house singers, including Frank Sinatra, Dinah Shore, Bea Wain, and Helen Forrest.

But more and more, records began to dominate the programs. Many artists were pleased to have their discs featured, but others objected to what they considered exploitation. In 1936 WNEW became the defendant in a legal action initiated by Paul Whiteman, Sammy Kaye, and Fred Waring. At that time, phonograph record labels carried the warning: *Not Licensed for Radio Broadcast.* The purpose was to prevent records from undermining performers' network contracts, which usually called for exclusive services. The court ruled that a broadcaster, having purchased a phonograph record, could broadcast it without further obligation, regardless of the wishes of artists or manufacturers. The warning on the label was held to have no legal significance. The ruling put the disc jockey for the first time on a secure legal footing. Ironically, the initial opposition of the artists was to turn in subsequent years into a desperate attempt to get the stations to play their records. WNEW's victory opened the door for all the country's radio stations to fill the air with recorded music.

Two of WNEW's musical giants: Merle Pitt, *right,* led The Five Shades of Blue, and Roy Ross conducted the studio orchestra.

I've been listening to WNEW since 1935. I always caught Martin Block every night. I believe he played the new releases on Friday night. I'd buy the records (Bluebird, Decca, Capitol, Columbia and Harmony) on Saturday. The cost—35¢ a record.
ANDY ESPOSITO

When Fanny Rose Shore arrived in New York, she landed a non-paying job at WNEW. Music director Jimmy Rich, *above*, sensed her great potential and arranged an audition for Martin Block. Shore chose the song *Dinah*. Introducing her on the air later, Block forgot her first name. Without missing a beat, he said, "Ladies and gentlemen, Miss Dinah Shore." "I was so grateful," Shore said recently, "that I never corrected him." Dinah Shore performed on several sustaining programs on WNEW, and sang duets with another young singer—Frank Sinatra.

One afternoon, my older sister came bounding into the house and called out to me "Hey, kid, how would you like to come over to Fort Lee with me tonight. Julie's brother-in-law is wowing the bobby soxers at the Paramount Theater in New York, and we have been invited to his apartment tonight." With the vision of a night owl I replied, "Oh, who feels like going way over to Fort Lee! I'd rather listen to some GOOD music on the radio." And so instead of spending an evening with Frank Sinatra, I listened at home to the groovy music set forth by Martin Block on trusty WNEW. I'm still eating my old bobby socks, thread by thread, to atone for my misdemeanor.
BEATRICE PEPPARD HERMAN

BILL HENRI
AND
HIS
HEADLINERS

WNEW

When Frank Sinatra performed on WNEW in 1939, Bernice Judis refused to pay his carfare. Discouraged, Sinatra got a job as master of ceremonies, headwaiter, and sometime singer at the Rustic Cabin, a roadhouse near Alpine, NJ. WNEW carried live broadcasts from the Rustic Cabin on the evening *Dance Parade* program. One night, a former trumpeter in Benny Goodman's band, named Harry James, heard the show and called the station for the singer's name. James had started his own band and was looking for a vocalist. He stopped at the Rustic Cabin to hear Sinatra, and signed him up.

WESTERN UNION

NAC5 16MW HAVERSTRAW DEPOT NY 13 852A

AUG 13 AM 9 14

STAN SHAW=

WNEW 501 MADISON AVE=

STAN HOW ABOUT A GUY LOMBARDO NUMBER AT SIX OCLOCK MONDAY

MORNING AND DONT FORGET THE WEATHER REPORTS=

=FRENCHIE THE FARMER=

SHORTLY AFTER THAT LAND-mark decision, WNEW became the first station to broadcast around the clock, and Stan Shaw became New York's only all-night DJ. The name *Milkman's Matinee* is commonly attributed to Walter Winchell. The show quickly became a success.

Life, October 23, 1939:

"On the night shift in New York's metropolitan area, more than 400,000 people keep the vigil until dawn. They are police sergeants at their desks in precinct houses, charwomen scrubbing floors, bakers working at their ovens, tugboat crews out to meet an early freighter, tired cabbies waiting for another fare. As their vigil turns to boredom, most of them switch on radios, tune to WNEW, the only Manhattan station on the air all night, to hear the *Milkman's Matinee.* Radio's longest program, it fills the lonely hours between 2 and 7 A.M., six days a week, with an endless stream of request recordings and cheery ad lib.

"Conductor of the program, on terms of big-city intimacy with his listeners, is Stan Shaw, 'Your very good friend the

Stan Shaw, *left,* **changes records with his assistant John Flora by double-tossing two records into mid-air at once. Breakage was at a minimum.**

Millie of Postal (Myldred Enright) took telegram requests. Hearing Shaw's ecstatic praises, listeners imagined her a glamorous figure.

Milkman. To fill their 100 to 250 requests that thump in on two teletype machines installed in the studio, Stan and his assistant, John Flora, riffle through a library of 10,000 records, play an average of 80 in their five hours on the air. The program's only set piece is *Liebestraum*, which Stan introduces around 4:30 A.M. with a tender dedication in Spanish to his Spanish dancer wife, Gloria Garcia.

"Proprietors of gathering places for his audience have found that the price of a telegram nets them a cheap and effective form of radio advertising. The effectiveness of Stan's program is further attested by the fact that similar programs have sprung up in other U.S. big cities. But he is proudest of his three public services. For farmers and fishermen he intones weather reports and market news. For the police he reads descriptions of missing persons, which have helped locate 17 so far. And for sleepless patients in at least one New York hospital, Stan's soothing records have cut down on opiates."

> *From 1938 until I went into the service, I would always get home in
> time for Martin Block at 5:30. My sister told me that my mother used to
> turn it on just to conjure up my presence at home.*
>
> THOMAS DOHERTY

Stan the All-Night Music Man, *The Night Mayor of New York,* brought millions of listeners to WNEW. Jimmy Rich attracted a large audience to his *Dance Parade,* and every morning Rosalind Sherman interviewed celebrities on *Guess Who Came to Breakfast.* Written and produced by Gary Stevens, the show marked the radio debut of Paul Muni and Barry Fitzgerald, as well as featuring appearances by Bob Hope, Bing Crosby, and Kate Smith. Alan Courtney hosted the *Joymakers' Club* every day at 11:30 A.M., with Tempo King a popular part of his show. On a jazz-oriented program developed by Bob Bach, regular panelists and guest performers like Charlie Barnet and Benny Carter fielded listeners' questions in a format modeled on *Information Please.* And every day at 5:15 P.M. Richard Brooks offered news and commentary.

One popular show would seem unsuited to the radio medium. *Here's Looking at You* featured Richard Willis giving advice on make-up and grooming. John Van Buren Sullivan remembers: "If there ever was a visual show, it was this one. But Richard Willis was good, and he and Judis would fight like cats and dogs. 'What the hell do you mean a pastel? What color pastel? What is pastel? That's an adjective.' But that show ran for years. Especially when he had that studio the orchestra performed in, he filled that every day."

BENNY GOODMAN WON *Metronome's* 1938 Dance Band Contest, as he had done in 1937. Hal Kemp was the number one Sweet Band, also retaining his title from the previous year. The song most played on New York radio in June 1938 was *This Time It's for Real.*

Martin Block's celebrity continued to grow, and he became strongly associated with the Big Band sound. Block hosted many live appearances by the bands, and in 1938 he assembled the largest live concert ever held in New York. Here is an account from the July issue of *Metronome:*

"A gala day for the jitterbug, alligator, cat and all the menagerie of swing was Sunday, May 29, when Martin Block presented his colossal Carnival of Swing at Randall's Island Stadium.

"Weather was swell, except for the wind that sometimes carried the music off, giving a fade-out effect like a transoceanic broadcast. Also tough on vocals and gag lines. But it didn't rain, so what the hell?

"Attendance bettered the 25,000 mark....

"Presentation moved fast. Huge stage permitted two full bands to set up at once with room for smaller outfits in the middle. That way, while one band swung out, another was always in preparation. Length of show didn't seem to worry anyone. Entire gang stuck to their seats from around ten in the morning until nearly five in the afternoon, during which time over thirty bands (leaders and full personnel) appeared.

"Applause was lavish for everyone, but emphasis was noted after Duke

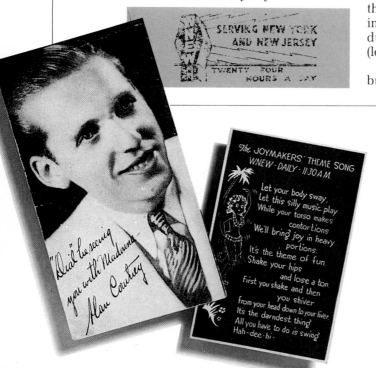

Growing up in a small town in South Jersey, we did not receive the New York stations. However, one Saturday morning my radio dial shifted and a very staticy Martin Block came on. On that day a young girl became hooked, both on WNEW and the Big Band era. Somehow, only on Saturday did we receive the station, and so, every Saturday morning, I would pull up my chair to the radio, put my ear to it, and listen enraptured.

GLORIA KUSHNER

Ellington, Larry Clinton, Count Basie, Chick Webb (with Ella Fitzgerald), Will Hudson, and, of course, Gene Krupa who closed the bill.

"Surprise item was Rudy Vallee who wowed them with his non-swing *Butcher Boy.* Kay Kyser was welcomed with roars....

"Space doesn't permit listing all the leaders who rallied 'round to this benefit for New York's Local 802, but rest assured everybody available turned out and gave their best. The Carnival of Swing should go down in history as a classic example of the real popularity of jazz music and its makers."

Martin Block welcomes Count Basie to the 1938 Carnival of Swing on Randall's Island.

The year was 1940 and my grocer boss and I were listening to Martin Block. Martin played a song called "Where Oh Where Has My Little Dog Gone" and he commented that he had received several letters admonishing him for playing such music using undesirable language. "Doggone." Things have surely changed.

SAL SPADAFORA

NEW YORK MADE 'EM—LOVES 'EM—LISTENS TO 'EM
ON WNEW 24 hours a day— 7 days a week!

From Ann to Zeke—They Hold the Key to World's Richest Market!

ANN PERRY — Song Stylist

JOHN B. KENNEDY
Noted News Analyst

ZEKE MANNERS
America's No. 1 Hillbilly

BOB CONSIDINE
"On The Line"
— Sports

THESE artist-salesmen talk the language of the city. They are *warm friends* to New York's millions—nursed, doted upon, *accepted* as very special proteges. No wonder—when these entertainers tell of your products over WNEW—your goods *move fast at lowest cost of any station in the metropolitan trading area!*

WNEW's VAST LISTENING AUDIENCE

Independent surveys prove that—*in and around New York more people listen to WNEW than any other independent station.* Additional proof indeed, that: WNEW is your best bet in the world's richest market!

1130 on Your Dial WNEW New York

Serving New York and New Jersey—Represented Nationally by John Blair & Co.

MARTIN BLOCK
"Make-Believe Ballroom"

KATHRYN CRAVENS
"News Thru A Woman's Eyes"

STAN SHAW
A New York Institution
"Milkman's Matinee"

FRANK FROEBA — Pianologist

One episode I remember was during the first year of World War II when Martin Block asked his listeners for old, used or new pianos for the various U.S.O. clubs. With Martin's great salesmanship and his fantastic rapport with his listeners, needless to say, he got quite a few.
JOE TIRONE

600,000 votes were cast in the January-February 1939 Make Believe Ballroom Orchestra Popularity Poll. The results: Artie Shaw and Benny Goodman tied for first place, followed by Tommy Dorsey, Glen Gray, and Sammy Kaye.

Metronome, October 1939:

"JITTERBUG RIOTS THREATEN WNEW SWING CONCERTS

"Jitterbug over-exuberance may bring to a sudden close the series of swing concerts sponsored by New York's indie station WNEW. Direct cause is a near riot that sprang up during the broadcasting of Count Basie and Eddie DeLange on September 19, each hep-cat trying to climb over the one in front of him in order to gain a spot closer to the bands. Result was a constant background clamor that almost drowned out the music and announcements, and which m.c. Martin Block, being on the air at the time, was unable to quell. Block, highly incensed, threatened after the broadcast to discontinue further concerts unless kids could control themselves."

POPULAR PROGRAMS DURING the Forties included *WW Ranch,* later to become *Zeke Manners and the Gang* featuring *America's No. 1 Hillbilly* in an hour of country songs and downhome humor. New Yorkers woke up to *By the Dawn's Early Light,* spent the morning with *The Music Makers, Make Believe Ballroom,* and *Keys to Happiness,* and tuned in to 30 minutes of *Luncheon Music.* Afternoon audiences listened to *The Singing Cowboy, Insurance Talk, Fashions in Music,* and

String Fever until *Music Hall* came on at 3. The Five Shades of Blue played live music every evening at 5. After the evening *Ballroom,* the nighttime hours were filled with 15-minute segments of music featuring such artists as Dinah Shore, Sammy Kaye, and Tommy Dorsey. Most people ended the evening with *Dance Parade,* but night-owls stayed up with *Milkman's Matinee.*

On March 29, 1941, WNEW changed to its present frequency, 1130 kilocycles.

WNEW was broadcasting news reports six times a day, including *News Thru A Woman's Eyes* with Kathryn Cravens. However, three weeks after the invasion of Pearl Harbor in December 1941, Bernice Judis issued an edict: "We've got to have more news. People are in this war, America is in this war." Jack Sullivan remembers: "She talked to the *Daily News,* and they set up the radio broadcast desk. Eighteen people compiled and wrote and sent it to the station by teleprinter, 24 five-minute newscasts a day. The station had final say in the editing, and broadcast them on the half-hour. Everybody else did news on the hour, and there was something about *7:30 On Your Clock, 1130 On Your Dial.*"

On January 1, 1942, WNEW News went on the air. The relationship with the *Daily News* lasted until WNEW created its own news operation in 1958. WNEW was the first radio station in the country with hourly news around the clock, and the station's new slogan became *Your Favorite Station for Music and News.*

Martin Block is temporarily overcome when he brings together the leading jazz musicians of the day for a live session in the WNEW studios. *Left to right:* Tommy Dorsey, Jack Jenney, Bunny Berigan and Roy Eldridge. Other artists who appeared include Harry James, Coleman Hawkins, Gene Krupa and Count Basie.

News Around The Clock
WNEW 1130 ON THE DIAL
Daily News broadcast schedule: REGULAR editions 24 times a day on the half hour. EXTRA editions on the hour, whenever news is urgent. BULLETINS at once.

During the Forties, "Block Dances" were very popular. We'd get permission from the city and rope off part of a block. The music was supplied by a phonograph and many 78s. These dances usually ended about 11 P.M. After we put away the records, we'd put on Art Ford and the Milkman's Matinee on our car radios and we'd dance on the sidewalk until 1 or 2 A.M.
AL MENDILLO

ART FORD TOOK OVER *Milkman's Matinee* in 1942, and the first song he played was *Moonglow* by the Benny Goodman Quartet. Betty Obrecht, in *Turntable Tunesmiths*, reports that Ford credits John Barrymore with his choice of a career in radio. Art had a one-line role in a Shakespearean play, and one night Barrymore came backstage. Ford asked his opinion of the performance. Barrymore gave him a long look, and quietly said, "Young man, as an actor, you'd make a fine radio announcer."

Ford was the first air personality to play complete musical scores from movies. At first, Art featured American films, but listeners soon became accustomed to hearing music from Japanese or Greek movies. A portion of his show might feature Haitian, Hindustani, or Swahili music, followed immediately by the music of Porter, Gershwin, Ellington, or Pee Wee Hunt. In an interview with Rex Lardner of the New York *Herald Tribune*, Ford explained:

"You always have to mix diplomacy with showmanship when you wander too far off the track. If I can get Chiemi Eri over here, I'll have to introduce her as the Rosemary Clooney of Tokyo. If I play a record by a quartet of Swahilis, I call them the Mills Brothers of Zanzibar. Swedish jazz and French vocalists are a little bit more acceptable. Partly because I've introduced the platters of so many vocalists here, Radio Diffusion Française has made me an honorary program director. Sometimes I persuade American lyricists to bang out American words to French tunes." Art Ford continued on *Milkman's Matinee* until 1954, when he shifted to the daytime schedule.

Santa's helper Barbara Nichols brings holiday cheer, among other things, to Art Ford when she visits *Milkman's Matinee.*

Way back in 1942-43 I was a young naval officer who had moved his young family—wife and baby—to New York City. After weather forecasting training at N.Y.U., I was sent to Bermuda. I had gotten used to WNEW's music while in New York. What a great comfort it was to hear my station again, which came in after midnight and lasted until dawn. It made me feel close to home and my dear wife and child who, I felt, were listening to the same music.

JAMES D. HOULIHAN

IN THE EARLY FORTIES, WNEW continued to add personalities to its line-up. Jerry Marshall, hired in June 1943, would remain at the station for 14 years, hosting *Music Hall* until succeeding Martin Block in the *Ballroom*. And one night in 1944, WNEW staffer John Jaeger was driving home, listening to the competition on his car radio. He was struck by the voice of a young announcer named Bill Williams, and the next morning Jaeger called to ask Williams whether he'd like to audition. Williams tells the story:

"I got off the air, I guess about 6 or 7 in the morning, and I came over to the city and auditioned with quite a few others. I was either too young to be nervous or too tired from doing an all-night show, and I got the job."

New York audiences were soon captivated by the warmth and low-key humor of William B. Williams, and for the next three years he held several time slots. One day in 1947, Bernice Judis walked into the studio while Williams was on the air. He'd taken off his shoes, and his feet were up on the desk, revealing bright red socks. The fastidious Judis was horrified, not at his informality but at the color of those socks. And on that day, Williams was fired from WNEW for a breach of style.

Ted Cott began his eight-year term as Program Director in 1943, hired by Judis to boost the station's public service broadcasting. Among his many innovations, Cott produced one program which significantly affected the role of blacks in radio. A series by the American Negro Theater, which ran on WNEW in the mid-Forties, introduced actors like James Earl Jones and Ruby Dee in serious dramas, adaptations of grand opera, and plays drawn from major fiction. In 1945, WNEW produced several musical programs featuring black entertainers such as Josh White, Mary Lou Williams, Pat Flowers, and the trio, Day, Dawn and Dusk.

JERRY MARSHALL SIGNED ON IN 1943. WILLIAM B. WILLIAMS ORIGINALLY JOINED THE WNEW TEAM IN 1944.

JERRY MARSHALL
Your host at THE MUSIC HALL over WNEW
2 to 4 p.m. every afternoon but Sunday,
at 1130 on your dial.

Fall 1943, and the war was going full blast.
Eight A.M. would be heralded by the strains of "Der Fuhrer's Face"—
my signal to head for high school in my bobby socks.
JESSIE LANG

WNEW

501 MADISON AVENUE
NEW YORK 22, N. Y.

July 5, 1945

Mrs. Anna Milano
4607 104th Street
Corona, Long Island
New York

Dear Mrs. Milano:

WNEW is happy to send you a recording of Corporal Frank Milano's voice, which we received from overseas. This transcription was played on Tuesday, July 3rd on our program, "These Are Your Boys".

We hope that you enjoyed hearing the broadcast and may we extend our best wishes for a speedy return of Corporal Milano.

Cordially yours,

Ted Cott

Ted Cott
Program Director

*It was November 1945. World War II faded into the pages of history
and the S.S. Jonathan Worth was steaming westward taking us home
to the shores we had fought for. One morning, still at sea,
the ship's radio was broadcasting over the intercom and I heard the very familiar
and warm tones of Martin Block. I knew I was home.
There was this interior surge and swell and dammit, I cried.*

AUSTIN FRANCIS

BROADCASTING TO A WAR-saddened New York during World War II, WNEW offered music to soften the war news, but also presented many programs of community service. One feature, developed by Ted Cott, was called *These Are Your Boys,* compiled from special material sent directly from battle fronts all over the world. The station sent out postcards informing people when news of their loved ones would be broadcast.

Sometimes, help for the war effort came unexpectedly. Martin Block told of the day he was handed a new recording by a "cute little fellow with a pancake hat" who was waiting backstage: "I took the record over to the studio and I put it on and I played it and it was hysterical! And the minute I played it the telephone rang. 'Play it again, play it again.' Suddenly, the thought came to me, why should I play it for nothing? If

it's that funny I can get money for it or a bond.

"So on the air I said, 'As soon as I have sold $5,000 worth of war bonds, I'll play it again. Well, the phone started lighting up, 'I'll take 100, I'll take 50, I'll take 500.' 'Okay, we have $5,000, here we go again with *Der Fuhrer's Face* by Spike Jones.' I refused to play the record unless I got $25,000 worth of bonds. Well, within one week we played that record 50 times. We sold a quarter of a million dollars worth of bonds, and made Spike Jones the most popular man in the United States."

The WNEW signal was so strong that pilots returning with troops at the end of the war used the frequency as a guide to fly into New York. Pete Johnson, long-time WNEW engineer, explains that since the signal is beamed northeast, pilots followed it directly to the airfield, listening to WNEW all the way home.

Martin Block's postcards to servicemen overseas were a welcome voice from home.

*I was expecting my first child. I had WNEW on as usual. I was making the
bed, and my husband was in the bathroom. Rayburn and Finch were
playing the song "Melancholy Baby" and they put a sound track of a baby
crying while the song was playing. My husband came running out of the
bathroom, because he thought I had the baby.*

GLORIA DONADIO

I
N 1946 THE STATION INTRO-
duced the first two-man morning
team in radio. Jack Lescoulie and
Gene Rayburn gave the city a new
way to wake up with their irreverent
commentary between records. Six
months later, *Scream and Dream with
Jack and Gene* became *Anything Goes
with Gene Rayburn and Dee Finch*, and
the pair went on to revolutionize
morning radio. Rayburn and Finch
were young unknown announcers
when Bernice Judis "married them to
each other" and allowed them to in-
dulge in a little horseplay. They were
the first air personalities in the country
to kid the commercials, and after the
initial shock, advertisers and audience
loved it.

Sometimes, however, Rayburn and
Finch got a little carried away. Once
when they were overstraining themselves, a phone call from Judis straight-
ened them out: "Listen, you big fat
geniuses, remember that a little joke
goes a long way at this hour of the
morning."

Walter Winchell, who usually wrote
his daily newspaper column while listening to Rayburn and Finch, referred
to the pair as "literate gabbers." Their
iconoclastic, hilarious antics were spon-
taneous, and their zany interchanges re-
flected the enjoyment they took in each
other. "We ad libbed everything," Gene
Rayburn reveals. "We said anything
that came into our heads. We lived our
lives openly, in front of an open mike."
Radio was never the same after Rayburn and Finch. They were widely copied, serving as the inspiration for teams
throughout the country.

Jack Lescoulie
and Gene Rayburn.

I began listening to WNEW back around 1947 when Art Ford was the Milkman and when all-night radio was practically unheard of in this part of Canada. Reception was exceptionally good on this small island on Canada's East Coast, and I tuned in faithfully, seldom missing "The Milkman's Matinee."

MICHAEL F. HENNESSEY

When Rayburn and Finch set out to demonstrate their ability to create hit songs on the air, they asked a music publisher for the worst song he could find. Playing the recording five times a day, they generated tremendous popular demand. Rayburn and Finch commissioned a full orchestral arrangement and produced a new version featuring a young singer just out of high school. *Music! Music! Music!* sold over a million copies and made a star out of Theresa Brewer. To prove that it wasn't a fluke, Rayburn and Finch did the same thing with *Hopscotch Polka*, which also sold millions.

WNEW was outgrowing its offices on Madison Avenue. Biow and Bulova spent over $1 million to construct new studios, and in 1947 the station moved to 565 Fifth Avenue. For the next twenty-two years, large golden call letters on the second floor balcony caught the eyes of passersby.

NEW YORK IN THE FORTIES WAS the magnet, the hub of the entertainment world. Orchestras played at hotel ballrooms, elegant clubs, and giant theaters. Glamorous Manhattan nightlife revolved around jazz joints and bistros from the Village to Harlem. WNEW was the station of the stars. Most major performers would not open a nightclub engagement or theatrical appearance without first coming on the station for an interview. Celebrities filled the studio every evening.

WNEW provided something for every listener. On Sunday mornings, children knew that when Merle Evans and his Circus Band began to play

Art Ford held a "Welcome to New York" all-night broadcast for Mel Torme in 1947. Among the celebrities who stopped by for the occasion were, *left to right*, Nat King Cole, Carlos Gastel, Torme, Ford, Stan Kenton, and June Christy.

Nursery Rhyme Songs, it was time for Henry Walden. News, public service programs, and sportscasts continued to inform. But above all, it was popular music that drew the largest audience, beating the networks against shows like *Ma Perkins* and *Stella Dallas*.

Bob Bach, writing in the April 1947 issue of *Metronome*, issued this warning to the networks:

"WAKE UP! THE DISC JOCKEYS ARE RUNNING AWAY WITH AMERICAN YOUTH....HOW COME?

"Have you, by any chance, heard the news about disc jockeys? Have you heard, for instance, about Martin Block's *Make Believe Ballroom* topping all your network shows at dinnertime? Another thing: do you remember any disc jockeys back around 1935 or '36 or '37? The truth of the matter, gents, is that the disc jockey is a phenomenon of the past 6 or 7 years, and guess who made him what he is today? YOU did. You did it with your little red pencils and short-sightedness when you brushed off live popular music for the quizzes. But make no mistake about it, the disc jockey is growing bigger and *bigger* and *BIGGER* all the time!

"The young audience, the kids, are going to grow up and become your audience of 1957. Do you think they will hold still for that inferior brand of popular music that sneaks through here and there on your biggest shows? Do you think they will not notice the complete lack of any important modern music on your air waves? Maybe television will have arrived by 1957, and you'll have a much larger problem on your hands."

Henry Walden, a well known newscaster in the Forties and Fifties, was my uncle. He had a Sunday morning children's show during which he read the Sunday comics aloud. He was known to his audience as "Uncle Henry" then, but I felt that only my family could really call him our "uncle."
SANDY SCHONBERGER

A MUCH LARGER PROBLEM indeed. In 1946 there were 7,000 television sets in use throughout America. In 1947, 178,000 were manufactured and the audience was estimated at one million. In 1948, Milton Berle began on NBC, and New York theater and restaurant owners noticed a collapse in business at 8 on Tuesday nights. A year later, more than 3 million sets were made. In 1950, Baltimore became the first city where more hours were spent watching television than listening to the radio. The radio networks were clearly in trouble.

Before World War II there were 900 radio stations in America. Today there are more than 10,000, and the greatest growth occurred right after the war. Competition was intense, and the key to survival was specialization.

Unlike network radio which was forced to create new kinds of programming, WNEW remained with an already specialized, highly successful format. The station felt the early effects of television when business fell slightly in 1949, after steady yearly growth. A remarkable recovery occurred the next year, as sales and profits again climbed. Sales fell again in 1951, but the cause was not television but a flood of the Hackensack River which silenced the transmitter for several days. By 1952, sales and profits were again the highest of any year to date. Television held little threat because WNEW maintained a commitment to musical quality which the new medium would never make.

Bernice Judis saw television as "just another competitor," but a greater challenge lay ahead. As rhythm and blues became rock and roll in the Fifties, musical tastes began to change. Throughout the country, independent stations adopted Top 40 formulas, but WNEW stood firm in its "good music" format. The station's resistance to rock would lessen in the next decades, with almost disastrous results.

WNEW SURVIVED THE THREAT OF TELEVISION AND STOOD FIRM AGAINST CHANGING MUSICAL TIDES.

In 1950 or '51, Martin Block played a song called "Oh Happy Day" by Johnny Howard. Martin said that this song was so bad that if it ever reached the Top 20 he would eat the record. In two weeks it was number one. He was flooded with ketchup, mustard, salt, and pepper.
WAYNE RAVESE

THE BEGINNING OF THE FIFTIES brought a new owner to WNEW. Biow and Bulova sold the station in 1950 to a syndicate headed by William Cherry, owner of WPRO in Providence. Judis was a key figure in the transition, becoming Executive Vice President in addition to General Manager.

WNEW concentrated its most aggressive competitive programming during the daytime hours of 6 A.M. to 8 P.M. The station conceded the evenings to the major television networks, but during these less competitive hours WNEW offered unusual diversions. When extravagant giveaway shows swept the country, Judis countered with a satirical program called *Lose Your Shirt,* in which WNEW took money away from the audience.

Evening and Sunday shows featured top stars who were willing to perform for nominal fees because they were permitted to do something they wouldn't get a chance to do on the networks. When CBS suspended its Sunday afternoon symphony broadcasts for the summer, WNEW jumped in with an hour of symphonic recordings with Benny Goodman doing the commentary. In a series called *Play It Straight,* Milton Berle appeared in complete seriousness as Hamlet. Jose Ferrer did a series as a Shakespearean disc jockey playing recordings of various actors reciting soliloquies.

One of the last live music shows on WNEW was the noon program featuring announcers who sang with Roy Ross' studio orchestra in addition to introducing records and doing commer-

Peggy Ann Ellis, *left*, takes musical direction from Roy Ross on one of the last live music programs on WNEW, *Let Yourself Go.* Noted jazz pianist Teddy Wilson gave Bernice Judis piano lessons after the show. The popular program was originally hosted by Alan Courtney, and Ellis appeared with Gene Rayburn from 1948 until 1952. Ted Brown later took over the show.

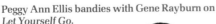

Peggy Ann Ellis bandies with Gene Rayburn on *Let Yourself Go.*

Bobby Hodges was the first Black radio producer of programs not specifically created for Black audiences. Hodges' career began when he wrote to Martin Block in 1937, asking for a job in radio. As producer-director, Hodges was responsible for shows hosted by Al Collins, Art Ford, and Bob Haymes.

WNEW 1130 ON YOUR DIAL

ON THE AIR 24 HOURS A DAY

cials. Bob Haymes, talented singer and songwriter, took over the show in 1953, and his wise-cracking style and unusual record selections brought complaints from the sales staff. Haymes recalls Bernice Judis' reaction: "She came in and said, 'Leave him alone.' She pointed a finger at me and said, 'Bob, you've got three months. You either get a rating or you're fired. Nobody will talk to you, nobody will bother you. Just do your own thing. Good luck.'" Haymes went on to great success, later leaving the show to Bill Harrington, another popular announcer-singer.

Another interesting show in the early Fifties was *Collins On A Cloud,* in which Jazzbeaux pretended to float high above Manhattan, reporting the sights below, with harp music playing in the background. Collins was a successful young announcer in Salt Lake City when he came to New York in 1950, hoping to audition for WNEW. He remembers the first time he met Bernice Judis:

"I went around to the back of the place, and there she was in her office, which was diamond shaped and the elongated ends were coming toward you and ending where she was. So you walked across 25 feet of carpet to get to where she's sitting behind a big desk with a light shining down on her.

"I walked in and I was about halfway across the carpet, she pointed at my beard. She said, 'What the hell is that?' I said 'That's my beard. I grew it out in Salt Lake City for Pioneer Day and I just kept it.' I said, 'If you don't like it I could shave it off right away.' She said to me, 'I wouldn't give a damn if your entire body and face were covered with hair,

do you talk like that all the time?' I said 'Yeah, I do.' She said, 'Well, I'd like to have you join our station. Can you start Thursday?'"

Collins started that week. He continues the story: "The first night I went to work, I was assigned to Studio 1, and I went in there and the entire studio was purple. I got on the air at 9:35, and I don't know where it came from, but I said, 'This is Jazzbeaux and I'm in the Purple Grotto.' And I had my Nat Cole going underneath it, the piano music, and I said, 'Yeah, you know, I play jazz music, but you can't play jazz in a fluorescently lit air-conditioned studio, it's too clinical, there's just no atmosphere. And I came down here this afternoon, it's beneath the studios and it's really beautiful. It's a grotto.'"

Just as Martin Block had done with his Ballroom, Jazzbeaux created an imaginary world in the minds of his listeners. Soon he was sending out solid purple postcards, reputedly photographs shot with special purple-tinted filters, with the bold caption: *Al Jazzbeaux Collins at work in the Purple Grotto.*

A 1950 Nat King Cole concert in Birmingham set off riots, and Williams broke the story on WNEW when Cole called him at the studio.

Al "Jazzbeaux" Collins in the Purple Grotto.

PAX MAX

THE WORLD WIDE MAX

MEETINGS NIGHTLY 10 to 12 MIDNIGHT on WNEW

The bearer of this card is a genuine MAX and is entitled to all rights and privileges afforded to one of this lofty order.

By Decree of MAX MAXIMUS *Al Jazzbo Collins*

Gene Klavan remembers: "We always looked as handsome as we could. Judis used to say we're appealing to women and we have to look sexy."

N 1952, WNEW INCREASED ITS power to 50,000 watts. That year, Gene Rayburn moved on to television and Dee Finch found himself without a morning partner. Gene Klavan was a young reporter who had come to New York to audition for one of the new television stations. Told of the opening at WNEW, he was reluctant to audition because he saw his future in television. Three hundred people tried out for the morning spot, and Klavan was offered the job. "What the hell," he remembers thinking, "I'll go back to television a week later."

Listeners thought that the new announcer had changed his name to Klavan because of the similarity to Rayburn. They were completely unprepared for the craziness of the two men. Finch played straight man, and during the first week Klavan used dozens of voices and characters. Judis called him into her office and said, "You don't have to do every accent, you don't have to do every impression. Take it easy. Coast a little bit." Judis was on the phone every morning, giving direction, shaping the team. The 15-year partnership of Klavan and Finch was born.

Gene Klavan

New Yorkers formed a new morning habit, and the pair appealed to all ages. Vicki Callahan, Executive Vice President, Radio Division, Metromedia, grew up with Klavan and Finch, and she remembers that they became two more members of the family. "It was part of getting ready for school in the morning and having breakfast with your parents." Klavan and Finch brought to morning radio a new kind of wild, satirical, irreverant lunacy, and their style was widely copied. They remained together until 1968, and Klavan stayed for another nine years as "the first one-man team on American radio." Dee Finch died in 1983, and Gene Klavan spoke recently of his long-time partner:

"He was spectacular. He was more than just a straight man. People say a straight man, but he had a marvelous sense of humor. A great voice and a fetching laugh. I mean, if he laughed even I couldn't help it, I would break up. And basically, he was really a good actor. He ad libbed. We never prepared anything, even though I used to hope we would sometimes. He had a great understanding of what we were doing. We were two minds without any."

WNEW General manager Harvey Glascock brought Klavan, Finch, and Rayburn together for an evening.

Dee Finch

> *While attending college between 1949 and 1954, I wrote Ted Brown*
> *a letter asking him to play a song called "My Happiness."*
> *I signed the letter "The Boys from 3625." He was good enough*
> *to play the song and commented humorously*
> *"with their taste in music, no wonder they keep them in a cell block."*
> C. WARREN NERZ

Shortly after Klavan joined Finch, William B. Williams returned to WNEW. Still known as Bill Williams, he added the middle initial for its distinctive sound. Williams hosted *Music In a Sentimental Mood* from 1 to 2 P.M., as well as the morning *William B. Williams Show*.

Another newcomer to WNEW was Ted Brown. "I always wanted to come to WNEW," Brown recalls. "I finally decided to audition, and afterwards Bernice Judis said, "Send the guy with the sexy voice in here.'"

Ownership of WNEW changed again in 1954, when the station was sold to a group headed by Dick Buckley, then President of the John Blair station rep firm. The tremendous surge of television and the uncertain future of radio may have influenced Cherry's decision to sell the station.

AFTER ALMOST 20 YEARS OF unequaled success, Martin Block announced that he was leaving WNEW. Bernice Judis conducted a nationwide search for a replacement, but Block's successor came from within the station. On January 1, 1954, Jerry Marshall, host of *Music Hall*, took over *Make Believe Ballroom* and continued for three years with great success, his popularity often surpassing the competing Arthur Godfrey.

TED BROWN JOINED WNEW BECAUSE BERNICE JUDIS COULDN'T RESIST HIS SEXY VOICE.

On July 18, 1956, Dean Martin appeared on Jerry Marshall's *Ballroom*. The next day, Jerry Lewis showed up demanding equal time. When told that Martin had been on for half an hour, Lewis said, "Good, I'll do 35 minutes." He stayed on for over an hour.

You asked for him . . . here he is!

JERRY MARSHALL *bringing a new sparkle, a young, fresh vitality to your long-time favorite . . . WNEW's* **"MAKE BELIEVE BALLROOM"**

Same "Make Believe Ballroom" Time
10-11:30 A. M. and 5:35-7:30 P. M.
AND NOW—TO 12 NOON ON SATURDAYS

YOUR favorite station for MUSIC and NEWS

WNEW MAKE-BELIEVE BALLROOM

1130 | ON YOUR DIAL

Fast-moving Marshall welcomes Tony Bennett, Perry Como, Kitty Kallen, and Lena Horne to the *Ballroom.*

On our honeymoon, we drove around and listened to Martin Block. Our favorite recording was "Swamp Girl," by Frankie Laine and we adopted it as "our song." Imagine when we heard Martin Block—on Thanksgiving Day—play "our song" as one of the "Turkeys of the Year."

DANIEL D. SCHECHTER

THE MAKE BELIEVE BALLROOM BIG 10 RECORDS CONTEST 1935-1958

A TISKET, A TASKET
ELLA FITZGERALD

I'LL NEVER SMILE AGAIN
TOMMY DORSEY & ORCHESTRA

BEGIN THE BEGUINE
ARTIE SHAW & ORCHESTRA

TENDERLY
ROSEMARY CLOONEY

IN THE MOOD
GLENN MILLER & ORCHESTRA

TENNESSEE WALTZ
PATTI PAGE

WHITE CHRISTMAS
BING CROSBY

MY BLUE HEAVEN
GENE AUSTIN

NATURE BOY
NAT KING COLE

SING, SING, SING
BENNY GOODMAN & ORCHESTRA

Lonny Starr hosted *Music Hall* and Art Ford left the all-night show for *Ford At Four* and the evening *Art Ford Show*. Jazzbeaux replaced Ford on *Milkman's Matinee* and once he kept half of New York awake all night.

"I came in at 12 and opened my mail and there was a record from Cadence Records, it was the Chordettes doing *Mr. Sandman* and it ran about 2 minutes and 7 seconds. I said, 'Hey, this is very nice but too short. I'd like to hear more of that.' So I put it on again, and in the middle of playing it the second time someone called and said, 'Hey, you know I like that record. And when it's over this time, play it again, will you?' I said 'All right, I'll do it.' I played it 3 times and I said, 'Look, I'll play it as long as you people want to hear it.' And I played that record 55 times that night. The police station called up and said, 'People are calling, they want to know what's going on.' I said 'Nothing, man, I'm just doing my show.' Then after a couple of hours I would change the name of the record. I'd say, 'Here's Benny Goodman, here's Tommy Dorsey,' and I'd always play the same thing."

When Jazzbeaux returned ten years later, the first record he played was *Mr. Sandman* by the Chordettes.

The Buckley group, which had subsequently merged with DuMont Broadcasting, sold WNEW in 1957 to Metromedia, which continues to own the station. By this time Bernice Judis had left, and Dick Buckley took over as General Manager.

WNEW acquired an FM license to broadcast on 102.7 and beginning in 1958, programming was delivered simultaneously on both AM and FM. A

Sales Manager John Van Buren Sullivan, John Jaeger and Program Director Jack Grogan toast Richard Buckley, *third from left*, on his appointment as President and General Manager.

Al Trilling, flanked by Williams and Sinatra, began his career as Chief Record Librarian in 1940. In an average week, Trilling and his staff screened 75-100 new releases, classifying and filing records, selecting songs to be played, and often choosing hit tunes before they became popular.

separate identity would emerge later. The broadcast day began with Klavan and Finch, followed by *Make Believe Ballroom*, now hosted by William B. Williams. Lonny Starr followed at 11:35 with *Starr, Sinatra and Strings*. Bob Landers and the popular Losers' Club came on at noon, and Lonny Starr returned at 2 with *Music Hall*. Dick Partridge, Jack Lazare, and Jazzbeaux Collins hosted two-hour shows until midnight, when Dick Shepard appeared with *Milkman's Matinee* at midnight.

THE 1958 WNEW LINE-UP.

Top row: Al "Jazzbeaux" Collins, Dick Shepard, Jack Lazare.
Middle row: Gene Klavan, Dee Finch, William B. Williams, Dick Partridge.
Bottom row: Lonny Starr, Bob Landers, Bob Howard.

Louis Armstrong appeared on Jack Lazare's evening program after a special Carnegie Hall concert in which the two performed.

> *I remember when William B. would start his 8 P.M. show with "Good evening, world." We lived in Amsterdam, N.Y., at the time and the only radios that could pick up WNEW were car radios, so just before 8 we would go out to a car just to hear William B. introduce his show with "Good evening, world." That made our night.*
>
> LARRY SPINAK

NEWS HAD ALWAYS HELD AN important place on WNEW, with hourly reports increasing to news every half-hour. But in 1958, the station created its own news department. The orchestra disappeared and the big central studio was converted to a newsroom. Martin Weldon was the first News Director, followed by Lee Hanna. Early in January 1959, WNEW News came on the air.

WNEW organized the most elaborate news operation in independent radio. From the beginning, WNEW demonstrated that a radio station can have the resourcefulness to create its own stories. The station scooped the networks by airing the first interview in English with Fidel Castro, recorded in 1959 in the Sierra Maestra mountains of Cuba. WNEW News has gone on to become

Ike Pappas

James Van Sickle

In a photograph which appeared on the front page of the December 23, 1960 *Journal American*, WNEW newsman Rudy Ruderman shares a laugh with former President Harry Truman.

one of the most honored radio news operations in the nation, winning virtually every major award in broadcast journalism. WNEW won the Peabody Award in 1960 and, most recently, the Associated Press Award for the best regularly scheduled news program in New York, the 8 A.M. report, beating the all-news stations. The news department has included such distinguished journalists as Reid Collins, Dave Marash, Marlene Sanders, James Van Sickle, and Rudy Ruderman.

Ike Pappas, today CBS Washington Correspondent, came to WNEW in 1958 with little radio training. Pappas considers himself "the luckiest person in journalism. WNEW gave me an opportunity to work with the very best people in the business. It gave me an idea of what the best is, and to emulate it."

Carl Brazell, President, Radio Division, Metromedia, remembers his days at a radio station in Houston. One of the newsmen was Dan Rather, and the two men met again on a New York street corner when Brazell came to WNEW. "We hadn't talked to each other for a couple of years, and he said, 'What are you doing?' I said, 'I just came up from Washington. I'm the News Director of WNEW.' And he said, 'You couldn't be with a better station. I listen to that news every morning.'"

John W. Kluge, President of Metromedia, has said, "Give us the right people, the best people, and we'll give them the authority and the autonomy to do their jobs the way they should be done." One of Kluge's first acts as President was the appointment of John Van Buren Sullivan as General Manager in 1959.

Marlene Sanders

Reid Collins

WNEW IS TRULY AN INTERNATIONAL STATION, RECEIVING RECEPTION REPORTS FROM LISTENERS IN MANY COUNTRIES.

Will the real John Van Buren Sullivan please stand up? Celebrants at an August 1967 party honoring Sullivan on his 25th year at WNEW don masks bearing his likeness.

SULLIVAN CARRIED ON THE tradition begun by Bernice Judis, bringing to the station a flair for innovative programming, a commitment to maintain the high standards already set, and a talent for motivating his staff. George Duncan, Senior Vice President, Operations, Metromedia, observes that "Sullivan's posture and his philosophy was as much molded by his own character as it was by his association with Bernice Judis." Sullivan recently remarked, "I had great training, and if I hadn't learned something since 1942, Judis would have whipped me."

William B. Williams: "Sullivan had this marvelous feel for the New York ear.

He was also one of the best men in the world as far as relationships with talent were concerned. No matter what your problem, you felt you could go to Jack and he would sit and listen to it."

Jack Sullivan believed that WNEW's greatest strength was its on-air personalities. Ted Brown remembers: "He'd say, 'Listen, I didn't hire you to do time and temperature. People have watches and they know what the weather is. I want to know about you. I want to know how you feel.'"

"He made each guy an individual," Brown continues. "He said, 'That's why you're here. You're here to tell about yourself. Be interesting, interesting, interesting.'"

O KEEP WNEW "INTERESTING" to its listeners, Sullivan decided to broadcast the New York Giants. Yankee Stadium was sold out every Sunday, and New Yorkers were wild over professional football. "It was a natural," Sullivan recalls. "It seemed like a WNEW type of thing to do." So in 1961, WNEW began what would become a long association with the Giants. Later Pete Rozelle told Sullivan: "You people rescued radio football."

Marty Glickman, who had been broadcasting for the Giants since 1948, came to WNEW and for ten years provided spellbinding play-by-play coverage, in addition to nightly sports recaps. Chip Cipolla first came to the station in 1958, hired as a field reporter for the newly-formed news department. Cipolla became Sports Director in 1967, and remained at WNEW until 1979. Al DeRogatis handled the commentary along with Glickman during one of the greatest eras of pro football.

New York sports fans quickly came to depend on WNEW. Home games were blacked out on television, and sometimes as many as 60% of the New York radio audience tuned in to WNEW on Sunday afternoons. During television coverage of out-of-town games, many people turned down the sound and listened to Glickman and DeRogatis. Fans attending games at Yankee Stadium would regularly bring along their radios. Al DeRogatis tells this story:

"I remember one experience in particular, a very tight game for the Giants, and Sullivan was standing behind us. The Giants put in Andy Robustelli, a tight end. It looked like they were going to go for a field goal, except I saw Andy look at Ralph Gugliomi. I turned to Sullivan and I said, 'They're going to fake the field goal and throw a pass for a touchdown.' Jack said, 'Say it.' In those days so many people were carrying radios to the game that I said, 'I can't do it. Because if everybody yells fake field goal, we just blew the game for the Giants.'"

Former All-American and Giants star Kyle Rote was Sports Director of WNEW when the station began broadcasting Giants games. Formerly, sportscasters were required only to report

Ted Brown, *center*, adds his inimitable charm to a Giants broadcast.

Former N.Y. Giants star Sam Huff, *center*, joined the WNEW sports team of Chip Cipolla, *left*, and Marty Glickman.

Al DeRogatis

Kyle Rote

what was happening on the field, but Rote brought to broadcasting the insight and experience gained from his participation as a player. Rote was the first of several former athletes to broadcast on WNEW. Sam Huff, after eight seasons with the Giants, came to WNEW in the Sixties and hosted the post-game show. Today, another former Giants star, Dick Lynch, hosts pre-game and post-game shows, in addition to providing in-game commentary. Lynch is joined by Jim Gordon, known for the past nine years as the *Voice of the*

Giants.

Kyle Rote has a low-key, affable style, and Klavan and Finch were particularly fond of trying to break him up during Rote's sportscasts. Kyle was the perfect foil, responding quickly with flustered laughter. Over the years, the pair did everything they could to interrupt Rote's delivery, from walking around naked to bursting balloons over his head to having hands come out of the air vents holding martinis. One day, Rote decided to get even. He secretly taped his sportscast for the day and while it was playing over the air, pretended to deliver his morning report. As soon as he opened his mouth, Klavan and Finch began their assault. Rote slammed his script down and let fly a string of obscenities. Klavan and Finch were devastated. All the four-letter words going out over the air would ruin Rote's career. Later, Kyle let them in on the hoax. From that day on, Klavan and Finch never teased him again.

John Kennelly, present Sports Director, came to WNEW in 1976. He was hired by Jim Gordon, then News Director, who said of him at the time: "Kennelly is a bar guy on the air. The kind of guy that you walk into a saloon on a Saturday and meet and have a couple of cold ones and discuss and argue about sports." Kennelly brings a unique quality to his morning news commentaries, in addition to hosting the popular pre-game show.

WNEW has been the voice of New York sports since 1961, broadcasting the Giants, the Mets, the Rangers, and the Knicks, in addition to frequent sportscasts during the news.

Sports Director John Kennelly, *far right,* **with Dick Lynch,** *above left,* **and Jim Gordon.**

EMPHASIS ON PUBLIC SERVICE programming has long held an important place at WNEW. In 1960, WNEW listeners contributed more than $20,000 to the *WNEW–Brooklyn Fund* when an air crash reduced a neighborhood to rubble. Several years later, WNEW brought to the attention of New York editorials of Ira Harkey, writing in the Pascagoula *Chronicle*. The courageous Mississippi publisher pleaded for an end to racial discrimination. Eight hundred listeners ordered subscriptions to the newspaper. Ira Harkey's single-handed fight for reason and good judgment won him the Pulitzer Prize.

In the Sixties, WNEW News presented documentaries exploring issues ranging from Freedom Riders and the slums to psychiatry, astronauts, and the Twist. In 1961, James Van Sickle came to WNEW, joining the respected news team of Reid Collins, Henry Cassidy, and Marlene Sanders. By 1964, WNEW presented New York's most comprehensive news report, the *Six O'Clock Closeup*, anchored by Van Sickle and including reports by David Schoenbrun, Jim Gash's *Inside Story of the Local Scene* and Kyle Rote's *Closeup on Sports*. Lee Hanna, then News Director, wrote in 1963: "No listener will quickly forget Reid Collins' moving description as he watched the St. Peter's Square throng and caught the first glimpse of Pope Paul VI; or the electric excitement of Earl Ubell and Stuart Loory as an Atlas with a man aboard lofted away from Cape Canaveral; or Jim Gash's daily enchantment with the foibles of New York; or Ike Pappas' con-

siderable anger (and not inconsiderable fear) as he told how an Oxford, Mississippi, mob attacked him and smashed his tape recorder; or James Van Sickle's calm reassurance as he guided us through the awesome detail of the rapidly escalating Cuban crisis. WNEW knew that this was the direction for radio to travel. It had to bring into the home—to the listener—the feeling of what was happening to us as a nation, as a world."

In 1964, WNEW organized *Operation Schoenbrun* to inaugurate the appointment of journalist David Schoenbrun as World Affairs Correspondent. The station brought 20 journalists and guests to cover French President Charles de Gaulle's press conference announcing new policy on China. The journalists participated in a question-and-answer session with Jean Monnet, creator of the Common Market, and joined General Lyman Lemnitzer, Commander of NATO and of U.S. forces in Europe, for luncheon. A high point was a dinner at Maxim's with literary luminaries such as Janet Flanner, columnist for *The New Yorker*. The group left Paris for Vienna, where journalists met with Bruno Kreisky, Foreign Minister and later Chancellor of Austria.

WNEW instituted special programming in the days following the assassination of President John Kennedy. The station cancelled the scheduled Sunday broadcast of the Giants at Yankee Stadium, and suspended all commercials for the duration of the funeral. During the period of national mourning, WNEW broadcast only appropriate funereal music.

THE DISTINCTIVE SOUND EFFECT AT THE BEGINNING OF WNEW NEWS REPORTS WAS INVENTED 25 YEARS AGO BY ENGINEER IRVING WEINSTEIN. NEWS DIRECTOR MIKE PREELEE STATES: "WE'VE NEVER BEEN ABLE TO DUPLICATE IT, SO WE HOPE WE DON'T LOSE THE ORIGINAL TAPE."

World Affairs Correspondent David Schoenbrun introduced General Lemnitzer to visiting Metromedia journalists.

T O CELEBRATE THE THIRTIETH anniversary of the station, WNEW presented a four-hour show at Madison Square Garden on July 24, 1963, featuring one of the largest groups of performers ever assembled. In support of the Musicians Aid Society, the concert carried the theme *The Best Is Yet To Come.* 18,000 people applauded the artists, performing on two giant revolving stages. The show was hosted by WNEW personalities, and featured the Dave Brubeck Quartet, Vic Damone, Bobby Darin, the Tommy Dor-sey Orchestra with Frank Sinatra, Jr. and Helen Forrest, Jack Jones, Steve Lawrence and Eydie Gorme, Billy Taylor, and Della Reese. The entire New York Giants team appeared, as well as the Peppermint Lounge Twisters.

The celebrities appeared without fee, in support of their favorite radio station. "We had everybody," Ted Brown remembers. "All the people that we played on the air were there in person. Everything went well. It was a fantastic, unbelievable show. A really proud moment for all of us."

FILMS   VIDEO   TV FILM

VAR

NEW YORK, W

WNEW TOASTS

What Makes a WNEW Personality   ANN

The anniversary gala was so successful that WNEW decided to follow it a year later with an even larger show. On June 10, 1964, station personalities emceed a spectacular at the Garden to benefit the Greater New York Fund. Artists appearing included Tony Bennett, Sarah Vaughan, Steve and Eydie, Jerry Vale, Trini Lopez, Buddy Greco, and the Smothers Brothers.

ESDAY, JULY 24, 1963

30TH WITH GALA!

Life & Times of a 'Perky Little Indie' Which Evolved as 'Big W'

ASH '63'S

Musical lighter played the WNEW theme.

Billy Taylor

Buddy Hackett

WNEW continued to present the best in popular music during the Sixties. Seven nights a week, noted pianist-composer Billy Taylor hosted live studio performances by such jazz greats as Erroll Garner, Woody Herman, and Duke Ellington. Regular *Music Spectaculars* featured live appearances by artists like Ella Fitzgerald, Robert Goulet, Count Basie, George Shearing, and Tony Bennett. Buddy Hackett served as the regular Sunday night replacement for William B. Williams, and celebrity disc jockeys included Dinah Shore, Milton Berle, and Mitch Miller. Sarah Vaughan spent a week on WNEW in 1963, announcing records and even delivering commercials.

Promotion Director Nat Asch came up with the idea of using rotating celebrities to review theatrical productions. Tony Randall, Faye Emerson, Walt Kelly, June Havoc, Ayn Rand, and David Susskind appeared, and Ben Hecht reviewed Richard Burton's radical street-clothes production of *Hamlet.* Bennett Cerf panned David Merrick's *Martin Luther,* and so angered Merrick that the producer asked for equal time. He chose to review his own production of *Oliver!* Asch remembers: "He not only reviewed it, he reviewed it as only David Merrick could. A paean of praise, not only to that show, but to every other property that he had. He took full advantage of the 2 minutes, 45 seconds. And only incidently referred to *Oliver!*"

Celebrities also did station breaks and recorded holiday greetings. Duke Ellington lent his inimitable charm by announcing "WNEW is an elegant radio station."

William B. Williams and the elegant Duke Ellington.

I can remember, as a teenager, doing the dishes on Christmas night and listening to Willy B. and the Christmas party he was having at his home...and thinking that his wife probably wasn't doing the dishes for all those people. When Ted Brown was on in the afternoon, I used to listen to him as I was preparing supper for my family. Many times the potatoes got peeled to the beat and gyrations of "The Stripper."

LOIS M. ROMANO

Live Music Spectaculars featured such stars as Jimmy Durante and Sammy Davis, Jr. WNEW personality Big Wilson joins Jonah Jones, *right*, for a trumpet-clavietta duet.

Sarah Vaughan spent a week on WNEW as a celebrity disc jockey. Surrounding Miss Vaughan, *from left*: Ted Brown, Gene Klavan, Skitch Henderson, Jack Sullivan, Ed McMahon, William B. Williams, Dee Finch, Jim Lowe, and Program Director Varner Paulsen.

Sometimes my whole life passes before me in the span of a day—the song of my first date, first love, engagement, first baby....
ALICE R. HYNES

Fans followed Jim Lowe everywhere he went when *The Green Door* hit the top of the charts.

THE REGULAR MULTI-HOURED shows continued. Ted Brown began his 3 to 6 P.M. drive-home slot in 1962. Fred Robbins gave the *Robbins Report* on Saturday mornings and *Robbins Nest* on Sunday evenings. William B. Williams hosted *Make Believe Ballroom*, and in 1964 began a Sunday *Ballroom* from 6 to 7 P.M. On his first show, Williams aired a WNEW exclusive, a recording of the appearance at the station by the original Benny Goodman Quartet, with Lionel Hampton, Teddy Wilson, Gene Krupa, and Goodman. Wally King hosted the evening show from 8 to 11, and Marty O'Hara took over the all-night program.

Jim Lowe came to WNEW in 1963, and a few years later, anchored a popular show called *Jim Lowe's New York*. Covering everything from disco openings to murders, three field reporters ranged throughout the city. Audiences were delighted with Lowe's inquisitive charm and fascination with details, qualities which would endear him to late-night listeners when he took over *Milkman's Matinee*. It was there that Lowe introduced a subject for which he has become famous. "It was something I used to fool around with on the air. Long about 4 in the morning, I had people calling to answer questions. No prize then. But I got it started and to this day I don't know if I thought up the name *trivia* or not. But I was the first to popularize the name."

JIM LOWE
CAME TO WNEW
IN 1963
AND SOON BECAME
KING OF TRIVIA
AND EMPEROR OF
NOSTALGIA.

WNEW 1130

By the powers invested in me
as the King of Trivia
and Emperor of Nostalgia,
I hereby declare by these
presents shall it be known

Don Bessey

is hereby enshrined in the
WNEW Nostalgia-Trivia
Wall of Fame

Jim Lowe

We asked William B. Williams of WNEW Radio what he thought of rock'n'roll:

My memories of WNEW don't go back very far as I'm only in my mid-twenties. My friends are still listening to the rock stuff and that's nostalgia to me! Most of it sounds terribly dated. You guys are what's happening! A Fifties recording by Frank or Billie or Ella sounds like it could have been recorded yesterday. It's not memories to me. It's right now.
KENNETH ROSE

MUSICAL TASTES WERE changing in the Sixties, and performers who came to prominence in the Forties and Fifties were finding it difficult to maintain their popularity. While WNEW tried to stay with its former programming philosophy, the rapidly expanding youth market was eroding the station's audience. WNEW was willing to experiment with the new music, but only if it met standards of quality. While rejecting Chubby Checker's version of the Twist, the station played Twist music in a more polished vein. WNEW was the first station in the New York area to introduce the Bossa Nova, and even played some of Elvis Presley's more restrained recordings.

Jack Sullivan recognized that the station would have to reflect current musical preferences. In the mid-1960s he instituted a policy in which WNEW began to air those Top 40 hits which least offended his tastes. Sullivan tried to keep WNEW in the mainstream by playing Arthur Fiedler's version of *I Want To Hold Your Hand* and George Martin's treatment of *Hard Day's Night.* William B. Williams, however, refused to acknowledge the Rolling Stones.

During the late Sixties and through much of the Seventies, WNEW tried a variety of adult contemporary formats, most of which were unsuccessful. Jack Thayer, current Vice President and General Manager, attributes the station's difficulties to a lack of clear direction. "WNEW went through a very trying time," he explains. "They did not find an answer anywhere because they were afraid to give up what they had to plunge into something new, and they were afraid of the new because it was not their genre." George Duncan observes: "Where we started to fail was when we stopped recognizing what our role was and tried to become something else. The minute we became something else, we were no longer unique and we slipped severely."

During the Sixties and Seventies, advertising campaigns sought to give the station a trendier image. But the foresight of William B. Williams anticipated a return to proven standards.

We're no make-believe ballroom.

Through most of the Seventies, WNEW searched for direction. Programming changes made in 1970 cut back on music. *Milkman's Matinee* was shortened, and a two-hour sports show hosted by Marty Glickman came on from 11 P.M. to 1 A.M. Julius LaRosa manned the afternoon show, followed by Jim Gearhart from 5 to 9 P.M.

Ted Brown returned to the afternoon spot in 1972. Jack Sullivan recalls: "I knew I wanted to do something about the evening drive-time and Ted Brown was the guy because he was a WNEW personality. There are some people who are created to work at the station and help build it. Ted's approach, his conviction and intensity, are very fitting, and it was a natural for him." Brown stayed in the afternoon slot for five years and took over the morning show upon Gene Klavan's departure in 1977.

Over the years, Brown has developed a close rapport with his listeners. "One day," Ted Brown recalls, "a woman called and said, 'I'm getting married at St. Patrick's Cathedral. I don't have a father, and my mother and my sister and I have been listening to you for so long that we just feel like you're part of our family. Would you give me away?' And I said 'Yes, I'd love to.' So I got into my tuxedo and walked down the aisle as her father. And I'm still her father. Her second daddy." Brown continues to host the morning program today.

Another popular personality to return in 1972 was Jim Lowe. After filling in part time for two years, Lowe revived *Jim Lowe's New York* in 1974. The new format was not as elaborate as the earlier program, but continued to present fascinating interviews with Broadway personalities, popular music, and Lowe's trivia quizzes.

Bill Hickok hosted *Milkman's Mati-*

Ted Brown interviews Judy Garland in London for a special Mother's Day program on WNEW.

nee in the early Seventies. In the middle of the decade the name of the program was changed to *The Nightmare Show.* Bob Jones took over in 1976, and he recalls what happened: "I brought in my own personal copy of the *Milkman's Matinee* theme, and played 50 of the greatest records I could think of, starting with *Because Of You.* The next day the secretaries told me the phones didn't stop ringing all night. 'Who was that guy playing all that wonderful music?' Every time I did the show I called it *Milkman's Matinee.* And pretty soon, there was a *Milkman's Matinee* again."

Jones first came to the station in 1973. As a young boy in New Haven, he had listened to Martin Block, William B. Williams, and Art Ford. "By the time I was about 11," Jones recalls, "I wanted to do the *Milkman's Matinee.* It was always my goal." He continued in the all-night show until 1980, when he began hosting the evening edition of *Make Believe Ballroom.* Today Jones says: "What I know about music programming I learned by listening to WNEW, and about presentation I learned from Williams and Ford and Block." He carries on the WNEW tradition as evening *Ballroom* host today.

Jonathan Schwartz was revolutionizing the rock music radio world on WNEW-FM, and in 1976 he added a Sunday morning show on the AM station. But the new program was quite different from what his FM fans might expect. Schwartz concentrated on music from the Forties and Fifties, along with contemporary songs which blended well with earlier standards. He played the songs of Rodgers and Hart and Gershwin, Dave Brubeck and early Peggy Lee, and between records, delivered impromptu essays on composers, writers, baseball, and Sinatra. Schwartz never failed to surprise: on Super Bowl Sunday, he played only songs with baseball themes. But it was Frank Sinatra to whom Schwartz paid the greatest respect. Introducing a recording, Schwartz would announce: "In just one hour, you will hear the premiere of Sinatra's new album, both sides, for the first time anywhere on this planet." For as Schwartz' numerous fans can attest, there is little about Sinatra which Schwartz does not know nor care about.

Management sought to improve falling ratings by rearranging the station line-up, and in 1977 a major shake-up occurred. Bob Fitzsimmons replaced Julius LaRosa in the afternoon show, and Jonathan Schwartz took over the evening program from Jim Lowe. Lowe had been holding down the most difficult period in radio, the hours of heaviest competition from television. In addition, many evenings were given over to broadcasts of the Mets, which continued to hold last place in the standings. The reshuffling did little to enlarge WNEW's audience, and changes were clearly required.

JIM LOWE RETURNED IN 1972. BOB JONES JOINED THE TEAM THE FOLLOWING YEAR. JONATHAN SCHWARTZ MADE THE SWITCH FROM WNEW-FM IN 1976.

Bob Jones

Jonathan Schwartz

I have been a WNEW "addict"
for over two of my fourteen years....
DAMON MOCK

SINCE 1954, WHEN BILL HALEY and the Comets launched the era of rock and roll with their recording of *Rock Around the Clock*, American radio had turned its back on the great sounds of the past. Reacting in panic to the arrival of television, record companies and radio stations zeroed in on teenagers with the strong message: rock is *your* music. Top 40 formats were designed to capture the growing economic power of the post-war youth market. Older audiences were virtually ignored.

The dominance of rock music was briefly challenged by disco in the mid-Seventies. Although rock prevailed, it reached the end of the decade in a weaker form. New artists were failing to excite young audiences, and rock was falling back on its former giants. A small but discernible trend away from rock music was evident on AM stations. As the nation's population gradually aged, advertisers became more conscious of the economic strength of the over-35 market. And slowly, a resurgence of the old sounds was growing throughout the country.

George Duncan, then head of the radio division at Metromedia, decided that the time was right to return WNEW to its former glory. Searching for the appropriate person to lead the revival, Duncan looked for someone who understood and related to WNEW's halcyon days. In 1979 Jack Thayer was appointed General Manager of WNEW.

Jack Thayer has been with Metromedia since 1959, and came to WNEW with many years of experience in radio. He recalls those first days: "The sense of loss of purpose was probably the most prevalent among the people on the air. The irony of hearing William B. Williams introduce Bread or Meat Loaf while meanwhile he's on the studio phone talking to Steve and Eydie and couldn't play their records seemed very inconsistent with what the strength of the station was." Duncan and Thayer realized that WNEW's two greatest assets were not being used—the music for which the station had become famous, and the talent of the on-air personalities. Together, they set about to recreate the sophistication and literate elegance of WNEW because they believed that a place existed in radio for the classic popular music which the station had done so much to popularize.

"When we first talked about creating WNEW again," Duncan said recently, "it was predicated on nostalgia." The new format began as an experiment by

This page,
left to right:

Susan Murphy

Bob Harris

Ted Brown

William B.
Williams

Jim Lowe

Bob Jones

Al "Jazzbeaux"
Collins

Jonathan
Schwartz

Double   You,   Enny   Double   You,

I live in a nudist camp in New Jersey. I want to tell you that I wake up with Ted, I listen to William B., I love Jim Lowe, and I go to bed with Bob Jones. As a matter of fact, WNEW is the only thing I ever have on.
ANONYMOUS

playing swing music in a revived *Ballroom* hosted by Williams on October 6, 1979. Positive response led to a live remote broadcast from the Rainbow Room in November. WNEW got its old records out of storage, moved to new studios at 655 Third Avenue, and opened its play list to pre-1955 Big Band music, as well as anything new by artists of that era and contemporary material that captured the feeling of the period. And within a few months, WNEW was back in all its glory.

Jack Sullivan insisted on treating recordings not as museum pieces of wax and vinyl, but as "living breathing performances by living breathing artists." Thayer carries on the tradition of Judis and Sullivan, blending what has worked in the past with the immediacy of the present, striving always toward musical quality. Thayer sums it up: "WNEW is doing something wonderful—twice."

Jim Lowe became Program Director in 1982. He maintains that "it's very important that those of us who are talking sound as if we're in exact step with today's tempo. We cannot sound as if we were recorded in 1940."

Ted Brown remains on the morning show, carrying on the great tradition of Lescoulie, Rayburn, Klavan, and Finch.

William B. Williams hosts the morning edition of *Make Believe Ballroom*, and in 1983 celebrated his thirtieth anniversary on WNEW. Jim Lowe, Mr. Broadway, lends his special charm to the afternoon *Music Hall*, and Bob Jones hosts the evening *Ballroom*. Jones, one of the stepping stones to the future of WNEW, plays "the music I grew up with, the music I always felt was appropriate on the station." Jazzbeaux Collins continues the all-night legacy of Stan Shaw and Art Ford on *Milkman's Matinee*, and Jonathan Schwartz works his magic on weekends. Bob Haymes, Marty O'Hara, and Ray Otis round out the line-up, captivating listeners in the metropolitan area.

News Director Mike Preelee states: "You give me a small group of people who are really dedicated and devoted and I'll give you great coverage." Journalists Bruce Charles, Peggy Stockton, Mike Eisgrau, Charles Scott King, and Carol D'Auria form this nucleus. *Close-Up* has become an award-winning program covering topics ranging from the economy to social issues and cultural developments. Bob Harris forecasts the weather and Susan Murphy rescues commuters with her weekday traffic reports. John Kennelly's caustic sports analysis brightens any morning.

This page
left to right:

John Kennelly

Jack Thayer

Bruce Charles

Mike Preelee

Carol D'Auria

Charles Scott King

Peggy Stockton

Mike Eisgrau

E   leven-   Three-   Oh,   in   New   York

*I don't think of the music you play as nostalgia.
Are great operas nostalgia? Is Beethoven, Bach, or Mozart nostalgia?
Is reading a novel by Flaubert, Bronte, or Edna Ferber nostalgia?
No, these are only the best, having withstood the test of time.*
JUDITH ROSS

MUSIC REMAINS THE HEART OF the station, chosen and played with discrimination developed over 50 years. "In our scheme of things," says Jim Lowe, "there's a right and a wrong. I think it's refreshing to know that in an undisciplined world, there is an area in which there is good and bad." Jonathan Schwartz calls it "great classical music," and Williams voices WNEW's guiding philosophy: "We do not care how a record sells, but how it sounds." This commitment has led the station to produce frequent specials spotlighting individual artists and musical themes.

The renaissance of WNEW occurred as the nation was recovering from an angry decade of revolution and social change. The youth culture and rock dominated the music scene. Could a station survive whose revival appeared to depend largely on nostalgia?

Historian Les Brown observes a strong swing toward quality taking place in society. Using the popularity of foreign automobiles and specialty food shops as examples, he notes a growing desire for a better quality of life, including what Brown calls "the most artful of the popular music."

Once thought of as nostalgia, music of the Thirties, Forties, and Fifties has come to be regarded by many as evidence of the greatest period of American popular culture. One appreciates a Renoir or Rembrandt not because they are old paintings, but as masterpieces. Awareness of the music's enduring ap-

peal is evident in the current cultural scene. Lena Horne's live show recently toured the country to great acclaim. Mel Torme, Margaret Whiting, and Helen Forrest play at New York nightclubs and sell out every performance. The 92nd Street YM-YWHA is in its thirteenth season of *Lyrics and Lyricists*, evenings devoted to the giants of American music. And the Kool Jazz Festival consistently presents artists of the highest caliber to large audiences.

WNEW has played an important role in the revived interest in classic American music, both reflecting and responding to a changed musical environment. Younger listeners are beginning to appreciate the craftsmanship of a musical past they never experienced. Jim Lowe observes that two generations grew up without ever having heard of Gershwin, Porter, Rodgers, and Berlin. They went from *The Mickey Mouse Club* to the Vietnam War. But now, Lowe says, "The

Bob Jones greets Tony
Bennett, and William B.
Williams listens to
Margaret Whiting
and Jimmy Rowles.

I am 24 years old. Thank you for giving people the chance to hear some really wonderful music, especially the classic songs that people of my generation wouldn't have had the chance to hear or experience if it weren't for WNEW.
GERARD F. DONNELLY

younger people are saying, 'Hey, wait a minute, these melodies are beautiful.'" And Williams agrees: "I notice in the phone calls I get and the mail that when guys and gals get to be about 21 or 22, they suddenly discover love songs and lyrics. I think there will always be a young audience growing up into this kind of music."

THE FUTURE OF WNEW LIES IN both its young audience and the evolution of American music. "We need more good songs and good singers," says Jonathan Schwartz. And Jack Thayer concurs: "The past is our strength and the future is our potential. WNEW has always been the showcase for the best in American music. We welcome the great sounds of tomorrow."

"We can make a success just playing those same records forever, because they're that glorious," notes Lowe, "but I don't believe that's the answer. I want to continue in this genre. I want more of the same. I want to enlarge the borders but with the quality intact."

Lowe continues: "We're at a very delicate time right now in the history of American popular music. Somewhere out there is a Jerome Kern, a George Gershwin. There has to be a spark. We cannot play *In the Mood* for the rest of our lives. We'd be a museum if we did."

Without question, the need for such a museum exists. But WNEW is much more than a rich repository for music of the past. The station pursues a critical examination of current music, seeking compatible quality in an on-going commitment to the best. Contemporary performers and composers are creating new music, based on an appreciation of classic American songs. WNEW stands firmly grounded in the golden age of popular music, but with an ear finely tuned to all the beautiful songs yet to come.

Photo: Allen Orkowitz

Across the dial, the sound is
unmistakable. No other station plays
WNEW's kind of music. And nowhere
are the voices so immediately
recognizable.

The men who broadcast on WNEW
have different styles and temperaments.
But they share a tradition which for 50
years has made WNEW personalities
the best known, most listened to
professionals in radio.

Bernice Judis sought friendly, sexy
voices that tempted people to answer
back. John Van Buren Sullivan believed
in a close match between the
announcers and the tastes and
experiences of their listeners.

WNEW remembers. The seductive
intimacy of Martin Block. The literate
looniness of Gene Klavan and Dee
Finch. The legacy of Stan Shaw, Art
Ford, Gene Rayburn, and Jerry Marshall.
A blend of the best of yesterday and the
immediacy of today.

You hear it in the erudition of
Jonathan Schwartz and the enthusiasm

of Bob Jones. It comes through in the sorcery of Jazzbeaux and the encyclopedic charm of Jim Lowe.

William B. radiates warmth and a sense of delight. A listener calls with a joke, and Williams can't wait to tell all his other friends.

Ted Brown paints verbal pictures with many wonderful voices. Although he gets up each morning at 4 A.M., he enriches his show by attending the theater, seeing movies, reading, and observing the world around him.

They understand New York and the day-to-day concerns of their listeners. They communicate genuine enjoyment and interest. And they are united by a love of the music they play.

It's been said that if WNEW were to go off the air, thousands of cab drivers wouldn't show up. For half a century audiences have tuned in to WNEW with interest, with loyalty, and with love. They've tuned in to hear good music and the voice of a friend.

TED BROWN

5:30 A.M. TO 10 A.M. MONDAY TO FRIDAY

My father had a retail food market, and I worked in the store when I was a kid...always waiting on customers, waiting on women... "Take a taste, you'll love it!" That's all I'm doing now, the same thing. It's no different.

I lie to myself. I set the clock for 4:30, and then I push it ahead. So what I'm doing, I'm getting up at 4. I'll say I'm getting up at 4:30, that's not so bad. Most people get up at 5:30. But it's really 4.... You say, who wants to get up at 4? I love it. I turn on WNEW, and the minute I hear that music I can feel my blood starting to move.

Ted and Torme.

I would do the same thing if I were sitting home in the living room. I'm the same way with my kids. I'm just the same at home.

WILLIAM B. WILLIAMS

MAKE BELIEVE BALLROOM
10 A.M. TO 2 P.M. MONDAY TO FRIDAY

There's a beauty to radio, in that the imagination comes into play. If I put on an old Miller recording or Sinatra, Artie Shaw, Goodman or Basie, people can close their eyes and literally take themselves back in time to when they first heard Sinatra sing Night and Day or the Miller band play Sunrise or Moonlight Serenade.... There is great therapy involved in getting out of stressful situations by listening to music associated with maybe nicer days.

The chance of your doing a world-beating show every day is impossible. So people listen for long periods of time. Let's say one day I don't play the kind of music they want to hear or I don't say the things they want to hear, they will stay with you because they know, having heard over the years, that if I'm lousy on Tuesday I'll make it up to them on Thursday. They forgive you more.

I think if somebody awakened me out of a truly deep sleep at 3 in the morning and put an on-air sign in front of me, I'd probably start talking automatically.

JIM LOWE

MUSIC HALL
2 P.M. TO 6 P.M. MONDAY TO FRIDAY

THE
WNEW
MUSICAL LEGEND
AWARD

We hereby bestow upon

Sylvia Syms

a venerable musical legend,
this special achievement award,
for excellence in the
fields of recordings,
theatre, or cabaret.

In order to succeed in radio, particularly in New York, you have to have a rough edge. You can't sound like an announcer. Another prerequisite is that you can't sound like a New Yorker, because New Yorkers don't like their own accent. I've always felt that being from another part of the country has been a definite asset.

I think I'm the only person in the world who subscribes to **The New Yorker,** **New York Magazine,** *and* **The Ozarks Mountaineer,** *and understands all three equally well.*

The fellow on the radio is a little more effusive than I am and a little more extroverted. It's what I'd like to be, probably. My alter ego.

BOB JONES

MAKE BELIEVE BALLROOM
6 P.M. TO 9 P.M. MONDAY TO FRIDAY
6 A.M. TO 10 A.M. SATURDAY

It relieves me to learn that the nation didn't turn its back on the greatest period of popular culture, starting with Irving Berlin until the end of the Second World War.

We do a blend of that which has already worked and that which is immediate. We point in the direction of something we believe is good. We know we're talking to you and we know who you are. We can say without presumption we think you're going to like this.

AL JAZZBEAUX COLLINS

MILKMAN'S MATINEE
MIDNIGHT TO 5:30 A.M. MONDAY TO FRIDAY

In the old days they used to have a bow tie with an elastic band around it. It was pre-tied and you just put it around your neck, and they called them jazzbeaux.

I live in Mill Valley, California, with my wife Patti, and I've got three children…so we figured out a plan. Every night I tape my show, and the next day it goes out. She's able to hear the program…and when I come home on the weekend, I say, "Did you hear that taxicab driver Wednesday night?" She heard him.

JONATHAN SCHWARTZ

10 A.M. TO 2 P.M. SATURDAY
9 A.M. TO 1 P.M. SUNDAY

I use the Red Sox to stand for whatever team is in someone's heart.

I think it's criminal to go on the air without an intimate knowledge of every record by each of the artists. Not only one album but every album. Every song on the albums. Every note.

**IF MY LIFE
WERE A MOVIE,
WNEW
WOULD BE
THE MUSIC.**

DODIE WOLTHOFF

We gratefully acknowledge the present and former employees of WNEW and Metromedia, Inc. who gave generously of their time and assistance, and without whom this book could not have been created.

We wish to thank the WNEW listeners whose contributions enliven the preceding pages: Marian Ambrosino, Richard Antos, Buddy Basch, Donald L. Bessey, Doris S. Bousquet, Bee and Debbie Bradford, Tony Camisa, Anthony Cassero, Theresa Cicero, Phyllis and Arnold Cohen, W.D. Coleman, Faye Crapanzano, Joan D'Amico, Alfred L. Damm, Michael K. Diamond, Don and Louise Donahue, Ethel Eisenberg, Angelo Fantozzi, Ted Fleischman, Peggy Ellis Fried, Joe C. Friedman, Richard J. Garfunkel, Mildred Gennaro, Ellis Glauser, Gordon Green, Mrs. Thomas Hayes, Norman Heckel, Mrs. H.C. Henry, Phoebe Jacobs, Sammy Kaye, James Kerner, Howard Koslow, Ann Lemp, Jackie Leonard, Frank Lisoni, Constance Lite, Joe Mammana, Pasquale Mancini, Lisa Massa, Sean McCloud, Bob McGonagle, Felix J. Melleno, Henry J. Merkle, Frank Milano, Dorothy H. Muller, Tony Narkey, John A. O'Connor, Dolores Ottomano, William Pollack, Leo B. Porter, Victoria Raucci, Lila Roberts, Walter Rosenfeld, Marvin Rothenstein, Roberta Ruttenberg, Michael Ryan, Ann Schiff, Herb Shaw, Dinah Shore, Bob Sincerbeaux, Dan Singer, Mrs. F. Spagnola, Ruth Stek, Francine Stock, Mary Toritto, Rocco Trello, Peter P. Trozzo, William F. Twibill, Allen Urkowitz, Mark Neil Walden, Peter White, Cecile Wichman, Judith A. Woessner, George F. Worcester and Martin Zuckerbrod. To the many listeners whose contributions are not included, we extend our deepest gratitude. We would also like to thank the Broadcast Pioneers Library, the Federal Communications Commission and the Schomburg Center for Research in Black Culture, The New York Public Library.